John Stuart Blackie

What does History Teach?

Two Edinburgh Lectures

John Stuart Blackie

What does History Teach?
Two Edinburgh Lectures

ISBN/EAN: 9783337764494

Printed in Europe, USA, Canada, Australia, Japan

Cover: Foto ©ninafisch / pixelio.de

More available books at **www.hansebooks.com**

No. 57   25 Cts.

HARPER'S HANDY SERIES
Issued Weekly

Copyright 1885, HARPER & BROTHERS	FEBRUARY 19, 1886	Subscription Price per Year, 52 Numbers, $15

Entered at the Post-Office at New York, as Second-class Mail Matter

WHAT DOES HISTORY TEACH?

TWO EDINBURGH LECTURES

By JOHN STUART BLACKIE

ooks you may hold readily in your hand are the most useful, after all
DR. JOHNSON

NEW YORK

HARPER & BROTHERS, PUBLISHERS

1886

HARPER'S HANDY SERIES.

Latest Issues.

Other volumes in preparation.

PREFATORY NOTE.

THE following Lectures were prepared for the Philosophical Institution of Edinburgh, and were delivered, with the exception of a few passages, before audiences consisting of Members of that Institution on the evenings of 8th and 11th December in the present year.

EDINBURGH, *December*, 1885.

THE STATE.

I.

THE STATE.

᾿Ὥσπερ τελεωθὲν βέλτιστον τῶν ζῴων ἄνθρωπος
οὕτω καί χωρισθὲν νόμου καὶ δίκης χείριστον πάντων.
—ARISTOTLE.

HISTORY, whether founded on reliable record,
or on monuments, or on the scientific analysis
of the great fossil tradition called language,
knows nothing of the earliest beginnings.
The seed of human society, like the seed of
the vegetable growth, lies underground in
darkness, and its earliest processes are invisi-
ble to the outward eye. Speculations about
the descent of the primeval man from a
monkey, of the primeval monkey from an
ascidian, and of the primeval ascidian from a
protoplastic bubble, though they may act as
a potent stimulus to the biological research of
the hour, certainly never can form the starting-point of a profitable philosophy of history.

As revealed in history, man is an animal, not
only generically different from, but characteristically antagonistic to the brute. That which
makes him a man is precisely that which no
brute possesses, or can by any process of training be made to possess. The man can no
more be developed out of the brute than the
purple heather out of the granite rock which
it clothes. The relation of the one to the
other is a relation of mere outward attachment
or dependency—like the relation which exists
between the painter's easel and the picture
which is painted on it. The easel is essential
to the picture, but it did not make the picture,
nor give even the smallest hint toward the
making of it. So the monkey, as a basis, may
be essential to the man without being in any
way participant of the divine indwelling λόγος
which makes a man a man. The two are related
only as all things are related, inasmuch as they
are all shot forth from the great fountain-head
of all vital forces, whom we justly call GOD.

The distinctive character of man as revealed
in history is threefold. Man is an inventive
animal, and he does not invent from a com-

pulsion of nature, as bees make cells or as swallows build nests. These are all prescribed operations which the animal must perform ; but the inventive faculty in man is free, in such a manner that the course of its action cannot be foreseen or calculated. It revels in variety, and, above all things, shuns that uniformity which is the servile province of brute activity. A man may live in a hole like a fox, but his proper humanity is shown by building a house and inventing a style of architecture. A man can sing like a bird, but—what the bird cannot do—he can make a harp or an organ. He can scrape with his nails like a terrier, but, as a man manifesting his proper manhood, he prefers to make a shovel of wood and a hatchet of stone or iron. The other animals, however cunning, and often wonderfully adaptable in their instincts, are mere machines. Man makes machines. In this respect he is justly entitled to look upon himself as the God to the lower animals, just as the sheriff in the counties by delegated right represents the supreme authority of the Crown. But, above all things, man is a progressive

animal,—not merely progressive as the grass
grows from root to blade and from blade to
blossom to perfect its individual type of vegetable life, but advancing from stage to stage
and mounting from platform to platform for
the perfectionation of the race; nor even progressive as plants and fruits are improved by
culture and favorable surroundings, and what
is called forcing, or as the breed of sheep and
cattle is improved by selection. No doubt
progress of this kind is made by man as well
as by plants and brutes; but his most distinctive human progress is made, not by imposition from without, but by projection from
within. These projections from within are
what in philosophical language is called the
idea; they proceed from the essential nature
of mind, whose imperial function it is to dictate forms, as it is the servile function of the
senses to receive impressions. These intelligent forms, coming directly from the divine
source of all excellence, and projected from
within with sovereign authority to shape for
themselves an outward embodiment, constitute
what in art, in literature, in religion, and in

social organisms, is called the ideal; and man may accordingly be defined as an animal that lives by the conception of ideals, and whose destiny it is to spend his strength, and, if need be, to lay down his life, for the realization of such ideals. The steps of this realization, often slow and painful, and always difficult, are what we mean by human progress; and it is the dominant characteristic · of man, of which among the lower animals there is not a vestige, neither indeed could be ; for so long as they have no ideas, neither reason nor the outward expression of reason in language—two things so closely bound together that the wise Greeks expressed them' both by one word, λόγος—so long must it be ridiculous to think of them shaping their career according to an inborn type of progressive excellence. To do so is exclusively human. Hence our poems, our high art, our churches, our legislations, our apostleships, our philosophies, our social arrangements and devices, our speculations and schemes of all kinds, which, though they are sometimes foolish, and always more or less inadequate, deliver the strongest possible proof

that man is an animal who will rather die and
embrace martyrdom than be content to live as
the brutes do, neither spurred with the hope
of progress nor borne aloft on the wings of the
ideal.

Of the very earliest state of human society,
as we have already said, history teaches nothing ; but, as man is a progressive animal, and
the plan of Providence with regard to him
seems plain to let him shift for himself and learn
to do right by blundering, as children learn to
walk by tumbling, we may safely say that the
easier, more obvious, and more rude forms of
living together must have preceded the more
difficult, the more complex, and the more
polished.   And in perfect consistency with
this presumption, we find three social plat-
forms rising one above the other in human
value, duly accredited either by monuments,
by popular tradition, or by the evidence of
comparative philology.   These three are—(1)
The prehistoric or stone period, from which
such a rich store of monuments has been set
up in the Copenhagen Museum, and the existence of which is indicated in Gen. iv. 22 as

antecedent to Tubal Cain, the instructor of every artificer in brass and iron. (2) The shepherd or pastoral stage, represented by Abel (Gen. iv. 2), in which men subsisted from the easy dominance which they asserted over wild animals, and from fruits of the earth requiring no culture. (3) The agricultural stage, when cereal crops were systematically and scientifically cultivated, which, of course, implied the limitation of particular districts of ground to particular proprietors, and those agrarian laws which caused the Greek Demeter to be honored with the title of θεσμοφόρος, or lawgiver—a step of marked and decided advance, insomuch that we may justly attribute to it the redemption of society from the *vagus concubitus* of the earliest times, and the firm establishment of the family, with all ·its sanctities and all its binding power, as the prime social monad. To the priestess of this goddess accordingly, among the Greeks, was assigned the function of ushering in the newly-married pair to the peculiar duties of their new social relation.[1]

---

[1] Plutarch conjugalia præcepta init.

The fact that the family is the great social monad, as it is undoubtedly one of the oldest and most accredited facts in human tradition, so it presents to us perhaps the most important of all the lessons that history teaches—a lesson as necessary to be inculcated at the present hour as at the earliest stages of social advance ; and Aristotle certainly was never more in the right than when he emphasized this truth strongly in traversing Plato's fancy of making the state the universal family, to the utter absorption of all subordinated family monads. Here, as in one or two other matters, the great idealist would be wiser than God ; and so his philosophy, so far as that point was concerned, became only a more sublime attitude of folly. The importance of the family, as the divinely instituted social monad, depends manifestly on the happy combination and harmonious blending of authority and love which grow out of its constitution—two elements with the full development and true balance of which the well-being and happiness of all societies is intimately bound up. The fine moral training which the family relation alone can inspire we

find not only at our own door, in the fidelity
and self-sacrificing devotion of our noble
Highlanders, who derived their inspiration
from the clan system, of which the family love
and respect is the binding element,[1] as contrasted with the slavish system of vassalage,
the badge of feudalism ; but in the habits and
institutions of the three great ancient peoples
to whom modern Europe owes its higher civilization, Hebrews, Greeks, and Romans, especially the last,[2] the great masters of the
difficult art of government, who, to use
Mommsen's phrase, carried out the unity of
the family through the virtue of paternal
authority "with an inexorable consistency,"
the beneficial effect of which could not fail to
display itself in social life far beyond the
sphere from which it originally emanated ; for
obedience to authority is the fundamental
postulate of all possible societies. With the
family, if not absolutely, certainly with the
best and normal state of it, most closely con-

---

[1] The word *clan* is the familiar, well-known Celtic word for
children.

[2] "Nulli alii sunt homines qui talem in liberos habeant
potestatem qualem nos habemus." *Institut.* i. 9, 2.

nected is monogamy ; for, though instances
of bigamy and polygamy, from Lamech downward (Gen. iv. 19) to King David and
Solomon in the Old Testament history, crop
up here and there in the oldest times, and
even in the post-Babylonian period, without
any formal mark of disapprobation, yet it is
quite certain that the Greeks and Romans
were guided by a sound social instinct when
they held the practice of bigamy to be incon-
sistent with the proper constitution of a
family. What troubles are apt to arise from
a multiplication of contending wives and ambitious mothers the latter story of King David
tells in more unhappy episodes than one ; and
generally it may be laid down as one of the
great lessons of history that polygamy, in
every shape, is one of those acts of Oriental
self-indulgence which may be sweet in the
mouth, but has a very strong tendency to be
bitter in the belly, and therefore ought by all
means to be avoided.

By the instinct of aggregation, which belongs to an essentially social animal, families
will club together into townships or villages,

and townships will be centralized into states. Humanity without townships would degenerate into tigerhood, or whatever type of animal existence might express an essentially self-contained, solitary, and selfish creature ; townships without that sort of headship which the word State implies, would make society cry halt at a stage of loosely-connected aggregates which would render common action for any high human purpose extremely difficult, and, in the general case, as human beings are, impossible. Hence the centralization of the Attic townships at Athens in the legendary traditions of the Athenians attributed to Theseus ;[1] hence also the lax confederation of the earliest Latin states under the headship of Albalonga ; and, after the humiliation of that old stronghold, the more closely-cemented union of those states under the hegemony of Rome.[2] What-

---

[1] Thucyd. ii. 15. The Athenians went further, and attributed to the son of Ægeus the creation of their democracy (Pausan., *Att.* iii.); but this, of course, was only the popular instinct, everywhere active, which loves to heap all graces upon the head of a favorite hero.

[2] See the words of the Latin league, Dionys. Hal. vi. 95, contrasting strongly with the original collection of autonomous villages described by Strabo, v. 229, κατὰ κώμας αὐτονομεῖσθαι.

ever may be the evils connected with the growth of large towns, especially when, as in modern times, they have been allowed to swell to enormous magnitude without regulation or control, it is one of the undoubted lessons of universal history that the social stimulus necessary for the creation of vigorous thought, no less than the centralized force indispensable to great achievement, is found only in the large towns. The Christians were called Christians first at Antioch ; and, had there been no Rome to unify a little Latium, there would have been no great Roman Empire to amalgamate the rude barbarians of the North with the smooth civilization of the South by the force of a common law and a common language.[1]

The form of government natural to such infant states as the expansion of the original social monad, the FAMILY, is a loose but not unkindly mixture of monarchy, democracy, and aristocracy—the aristocracy being always

---

[1] The influence of the great city in centralizing the villages and making a state possible was in Greece philologically stereotyped by the fact that for *city* and *state* the language had only one word, πόλις. The *city* was the *state* in the same sense that the head is the body, for without the head no living body could be.

the preponderating element. In the single
family, of course, we have only the monarchical element in the father, and the democratic
element in the children ; but, as families ex-
pand into townships, it could not be but that
the heads of the families composing it, partly
from their age and experience, partly from the
force of individual character, should form a
sort of natural aristocracy, while the less notable and less prominent members would form
the δῆμος, or great body of the constantly increasing multitude of the associated families.
Below these three dominant elements of the
body social, there would always be found a
loose company of dependents and onhangers—
the class called Θῆτες in Homer (Od., iv. 644),
and in the Solonian constitution—who had no
civic rights any more than the serfs and vas-
sals of our medieval feudalism. The weakness of the monarchical and the strength of the
aristocratic elements in the early societies
arose from the original equality of the heads
of families, and from the jealousy with which
they would naturally look on any functions of
superiority exercised by any of their order

naturally no better than themselves. The
king, accordingly, like Agamemnon in Homer,
would claim the homage which the title implies only for purposes of common action ; and
even in such cases would always be kept in
check by a βουλή, or council of the aristocracy,
of whose will properly he was only the execu-
tive hand ; while the great mass of the people,
occupied with the labors that belong to an
agricultural and pastoral population, and un-
accustomed to the large views which states-
manship and generalship require, would come
together only on rare occasions of peculiar
urgency.

The element in that loose triad of social
forces that was first formulated into a more
distinct type, and endowed with more imperative efficiency, was the kingship. The power
of the king was increased, which of course implies that the power of the people, and specially
of the aristocracy, was diminished. And here
let it be observed generally that the progress
of civilization in its natural and healthy career
is the progress of limitation and the curtailment in various ways of that freedom which

originally belonged to every member of the
community. The tanned savage of the back-
woods is the freest man in existence ; next to
him, the nomad or the wandering gipsy, such
as may still be seen in their glory at St. James'
fair in Kelso, whose house is at once his dwell-
ing-place, his manufactory or place of business, and his travelling car ; least free is the
civilized citizen hemmed in on all sides by
police-officers, soldiers, sentinels, door-keep-
ers, and game-keepers, and the whole fraternity
of dignified but unpopular officials of various
kinds whose business it is to the general public to say No ! This accretion of strength to
the king proceeded first from his mere personal
influence and the general deference paid to
him during the continuance of a prolonged
and easily-exercised sovereignty ; all classes,
even the aristocracy, whose ambition is thus
kept in check and their perilous enmities
softened, feel the benefit of a wise head and a
firm hand ; but the party specially benefited by
the kingship is the demos ; for this body, from
its position peculiarly liable to be trampled on
by an insolent aristocracy, naturally looks up to

the king as the father of the whole family, who, on his part, feels his position strengthened and his respect increased by performing with tact and firmness the delicate functions of a mediator. But the great social force which operates in giving prominence and predominance to the monarchy is WAR; and, though war is unquestionably an evil, it is an evil only as death is, and a form of dying accompanied not seldom with an exhibition of more manhood than the experience of many a peaceful deathbed can show. In fact, as stout old Balmerino said on the scaffold in 1746, "The man who is not ready to die is not fit to live;" that is, we hold our life under the condition that we may at any time be called on to sacrifice it, whether for the preservation of our own self-respect, or for the integrity of the community of which we are a member. All great nations, in fact, have been cradled in war, the Hebrews no less than the Greeks and Romans; and it is only an amiable sentimentalism, pardonable in women, but inexcusable in men, that, in contemplation of the hard blows, red wounds, and gashed bodies

with which war is accompanied, will allow
itself to forget the hardihood, endurance, cour-
age, self-sacrifice, and devotion to public duty,
of which, under Providence, it has always been
the great training school.[1] There is no pro-
fession that I know more favorable to the
growth of noble sentiment and manly action
than that of the soldier; and to its beneficial
action in the formation of States every page
of history bears flaming testimony. War, in
fact, is the principal agent in producing that
unification so absolutely necessary to social
existence, but which is lost so soon as the
headship of the common father of the expand-
ed clan ceases to be recognized. Thus it was
under the compulsion of war from their Lom-
bardian neighbors on the west and Sclavonians
on the east that the petty democratic com-
munities, which after the disruption of the
Roman Empire occupied the Venetian isles,
found themselves, in the year 697, obliged to
elect a king for life, wisely masking his abso-

---

[1] ὁ ϭτρατιωτικὸς βίος πολλὰ ἔχει μέρη τῆς ἀρετῆς.—
Aristot. Pol. ii. 9. St. Paul also frequently in the Epistles, and
Clemens Romanus (Oxon. 1633, p. 48) refers to the military pro-
fession as a great school of manly virtue.

lute authority under the name of Doge or
Duke. And in a similar fashion the situation
of the Piedmontese, constantly forced to de-
fend themselves against Gallican and Teutonic
ambition, begot in them a stoutness of self-
assertion and a general manhood of character
which up to the present hour has placed them
in favorable contrast to the inhabitants of the
southern half of the peninsula ; and the manhood displayed by the Counts of Savoy in
asserting their independence against great
odds was no doubt the cause why, in the
Peace of Utrecht in 1713, their lords were
allowed to assume and maintain the title of
kings—a circumstance which gave rise to the
saying of Frederick the Great of Prussia, that
the lords of Savoy were kings by virtue of their
locality.[1] This is certainly true, not only of
Sardinia, but of all States that ever rose above
the loose aggregation of the original townships. It was the necessity of adjusting matters with troublesome neighbors that caused a
perpetual succession of petty wars ; and these
could not be conducted without a prolongation

---

[1] Spalding's *Italy*, ii. p. 284.

of the power of the successful general, which
acted practically as a kingship. The successful general in such times did not require to
usurp a title which the people were forward to
force upon him ; and only a few, we may
imagine, like Gideon (Judges viii. 22), had
virtue enough to remain contented with the
distinction belonging to a private station when
the grace of the crown and the authority of the
sceptre were formally pressed upon them by
a grateful people. So in Greece we find an
early kingship signalized by the names of
Ægeus, Theseus, and Codrus ; so in Rome a
succession of seven kings, more or less distinctly outlined, the last of whom, Tarquin
the Proud, stands forward as the head of the
great Latin league, and entering in this
capacity into a formal treaty with Carthage,
the great commercial State of the Mediterra-
nean. Closely connected with war, or, more
properly, as the natural development of it in
its more advanced stages, we must mention
CONQUEST ; that is, the violent imposition of
the results of a foreign civilization on the
native social foundations of any country.

Here, no doubt, there may often be on the conquering side something very different from a manly self-assertion—viz., self-aggrandizement at the expense of an innocent neighbor, greed of territory, lust of power, and the vanity of mere military glory, which our brilliant neighbors the French were so fond to have in their mouth. The virtue of war as a training school of civic manhood does by no means exclude the operation of many forces far from admirable in their motive ; and it is the presence of these unholy influences, no doubt piously brooded over, that has generated in the breasts of our mild friends the Quakers that anti-bellicose gospel which they preach with such lovable persistency.   But whatever the motives of famous conquerors have been, the results of their achievements in the great history of society have been most important.   The imposition of a foreign type on the peoples of Western Asia by the brilliant conquests of Alexander the Great, gave to the whole of that valuable part of the world, along with the rich coast of Northern Africa, a common medium of culture of the utmost

importance to the future civilization of the
race. The imposition of the Norman yoke
900 years ago on this island gave to the con-
tentious Saxon kingdoms, by a single vigorous
stroke from without, that social consistency
which the bloody strife of five centuries of
petty kings and kinglets among themselves
had failed to produce ; while in India the imposition of the most highly advanced mercan-
tile and Christian civilization of the West on
crude masses of an altogether diverse type of
Asiatic society, presents to the thoughtful
student of history a problem of assimilation of
an altogether unique character, the final solution of which, under the action of many complex forces, no most sagacious human intellect at the present moment can divine. On
the other hand, it cannot be denied that the
blessings which conquest brings with it,
when vigorously managed and wisely used, are
lightly turned into a bane whenever the power
which has the force to conquer has not the
wisdom to administer ; of which unblissful
lack of administrative capacity and assimilat-
ing genius the conquests of the Turks in

Europe, and of the English in Ireland, present a most instructive example.

The monarchies created in the above fashion, by the combination of old patriarchal habits with military necessities, however firmly rooted they may appear at the start, carry with them a certain germ of dissatisfaction, which, under the influence of popular irritability, seriously endangers their permanence, and may at any time break up their consistency. The causes of such dissatisfaction are chiefly the following :—(1) The original motive for creating a king, the pressure of foreign war, as war cannot last forever, in time of peace will cease to operate, and the instinct of individual liberty, which belongs to all men, unless when violently stamped out, will revive, and cause the subjection of all men to the will of one to be looked on with disfavor. (2) This feeling will be specially strong with the ἄριστοι, or natural aristocracy, whose individual importance must diminish as the power of the king increases. (3) A great danger will arise from the fixation of the order of succession to the throne. The natural tendency will be to follow the example of succession in private families, and recognize the right of the son to walk into the public heritage of his father ; but the additional influence thus given to the king will have a tendency to sharpen the jealousy of the nobles. And, again, the son may be a weakling or a fool, and utterly unfit to play the part of a supreme ruler with that mixture of intelligence, firmness, and tact which the royal function for its fair and full action requires. (4) And if, in order to avoid these evils, the elective principle is maintained, either absolutely or within certain limits, the tendency to faction inherent in all aristocracies, stimulated by the potent spur of a competition for power, will be increased ; and this factious yeast will work so potently in the blood of the nobles that they will either reduce the power of the king to a mere name, and change the government into an exclusive oligarchy, as in Venice, or they will even go the length of calling in foreign arbiters to heal their dissensions, which, as in the case of Poland, will naturally end in subjection to some foreign power ; or, lastly, they will dispense with the kingship altogether, and return to their original mixture of aristocracy and democracy with more firmly-defined functions and more reliable guarantees. (5) This result may be precipitated by some outbreak of that insolence which is so naturally fostered by the possession of absolute power; the sacredness of personal property and the reverence of ancestral possession will not be respected by some Ahab of the day; some young Tarquin or Hipparchus may cast his lustful eye on the fair daughter of an humble citizen; and then will be unsheathed the sword of a Brutus, and then uprise the song of a Harmodius and Aristogeiton, which will sound a long knell to monarchy, during the manhood of a free, an independent, a self-reliant, and a self-governing people.

The system of self-government thus introduced, as the natural fruit of the elements out of which it arose, would be a mixture of aristocracy and democracy, with a decided predominance of the former element at starting, but with a gradually increasing momentum on the side of the inferior factor in proportion as

the mass of the people excluded from aristocratic privileges by a necessary law of social
growth advanced in numbers and in social importance. Greece and Rome, or rather Athens
and Rome, present to us here two types from
which important lessons may be learned. In
both the discarding of the kings was the work
of the aristocracy ; but, while the germ of the
democratic element was equally strong in
both, in Athens, partly from the genius of the
people, partly from peculiar circumstances,
this germ blossomed into an earlier, a more
marked, and a more characteristic manhood ;
whereas in Rome, in the most brilliant period
of its political action, the form of government
might rather be defined as a strong aristocracy
limited by a strong democracy than a pure democracy, to which category Athens undoubtedly
belongs. In both States the aristocratic element
did not submit to the necessary curtailment of
its power without a struggle ; but in Athens
the names of Solon (600 B.C.), Clisthenes,
Aristides, and Pericles distinctly marked the
early formation of a democracy almost totally
purged from any remnant of aristocratic in-

fluence, at an epoch in its development corre-
sponding to which we find Rome pursuing her
system of world-wide conquest under a system
of compromise between the patrician and the
plebeian element, similar in some sort to what
we see before our eyes at the present moment
in our own country. To Athens, therefore,
we look, in the first place, for an answer to
the question, What does history teach in
regard to the virtue of a purely democratic
government? And here we may safely say
that, under favorable circumstances, there is
no form of government which, while it lasts,
has such a virtue to give scope to a vigorous
growth and luxuriant fruitage of various manhood as a pure democracy. Instead of choking
and strangling, or at least depressing, the free
self-assertion of the individual, by which alone
he feels the full dignity of manhood, such a
democracy gives a free career to talent and
civic efficiency in the greatest number of capa-
ble individuals; but it does not follow that,
though in this regard it has not been surpassed
by any other form of government, it is therefore absolutely the best of all forms of govern-

ment. All that we are warranted to say is, as Cornewall Lewis does,[1] that without a strong admixture of the democratic spirit humanity in its social form cannot achieve its highest results; of which truth, indeed, we have the most striking proof before our eyes in our own happy island, where, even before the time which Mr. Green happily designates as Puritan England, powerful kings had received a lesson that as they had been elected so they might be dismissed from office by the voice of London burghers. Neither, on the other hand, does it follow from the shortness of the bright reign of Athenian democracy—not more than 200 years from Clisthenes to the Macedonians —that all democracies are short-lived, and must pay, like dissipated young gentlemen, with premature decay for the feverish abuse of their vital force. Possible no doubt it is that, if the power of what we may call a sort of Athenian Second Chamber, the Areiopagus, instead of being weakened as it was by Aristides and Pericles, had been built up according to the idea of Æschylus and the intelligent

---

[1] *On Method in Political Science.*

aristocrats of his day, such a body, armed, like
our House of Lords, with an effective negative
on all outbursts of popular rashness, might
have prevented the ambition of the Athenians
from launching on that famous Syracusan
expedition which exhausted their force and
maimed their action for the future. But the
lesson taught by the short-lived glory of
Athens, and its subjugation under the rough
foot of the astute Macedonian, is not that
democracies, under the influence of faction,
and, it may be, not free from venality, will
sell their liberties to a strong neighbor—for
aristocratic Poland did this in a much more
blushless way than democratic Greece—but
that any loose aggregate of independent States,
given more to quarrel among themselves than
to unite against a common enemy, whether
democratic, or aristocratic, or monarchical in
their form of government, cannot in the long
run maintain their ground against the firm
policy and the well-massed force of a strong
monarchy. Athens was blotted out from the
map of free peoples at Chæronea, not because
the Athenian people had too much freedom,

but because the Greek States had too little
unity. They were used by Philip exactly in
the same way that Napoleon used the German
States at the commencement of the present
century. DIVIDE ET INFERA is the politician's
most familiar maxim, which, when wisely and
persistently applied, whether by an ancient
Macedonia or a modern Russia, will always
give a strong monarchy a decided advantage
over every other form of government. Sur-
round me with a belt of petty principalities,
says the despot, however highly civilized and
however well governed, and I shall know to
make them play my game and work themselves into confusion, till the hour comes when
I may appear as a god to allay by my intervention the troubles which I have fostered by
my intrigues.

So much for Athens. Let us now see what
lessons are to be learned from ROME. And
here, on the threshold, it is quite plain that
the abolition of kingship goes in the first place
to strengthen the aristocracy, on whom as a
body the supreme functions exercised by the
monarch naturally devolve. The highly aris-

tocratic type of the early Roman republic, unlimited from above by any superior power, and
with only a slight occasional check from a plebeian citizenship in the tender bud, is universally admitted. Plainly enough also it stands
written on the face of the early history of the
Commonwealth that the administration of the
aristocracy was marked in no ordinary degree
by all that exclusiveness, insolence, selfish-
ness, and rapacity, which are the besetting sins
of an order of men cradled in hereditary conceit, and eating the bread not of labor, but of
privilege, "*das unverbesserliche Junkerthum,*"
as Mommsen calls them. To such an extent
did they abuse the natural vantage ground of
their social position that, while the great body
of the substantial yeomanry, who shed their
blood in a constant succession of petty wars
for the safety of the State, were stinted of
their natural reward and degraded from their
rightful position, the insolent monopolizers
of all dignities and privileges did not blush to
take from the people their natural heritage in
the public land, and, for the enlargement of their
own order, to deprive the State of its stoutest

citizens, and the army of its most effective
soldiers. The irritation produced by this insolent and anti-social procedure of the old
Roman landlords, by the law of reaction common to all forces, produced as its natural consequence a revolt; for, as it has been truly
said that the blood of the martyrs is the seed
of the Church, no less true is it in all history
that the insolence of the aristocracy is the
cradle of the democracy. That happened accordingly in ancient Rome which Sismondi
prophesied might happen in modern Scotland :
"If the mighty thanes who rule in those trans-
Grampian regions begin to think that they can
do without the people, the people may begin
to think they can do without them." [1] So at
least the Roman plebs thought when, in the
year of the city 259, they marched in a body
out to the Sacred Mount on the banks of the
Anio, and refused to return to the city till
their just claims had been conceded and their
wrongs redressed. Their wrongs were redressed : conferences, concessions, and com-
promises, in a hurried and blundering sort

---

[1] Sismondi, *Etudes sur l'économie politique*, Essai iv.

of way, were made; tribunes of the plebs
were appointed, with the absolute power of
stopping the whole machinery of the State
with a single negation; and thus was sown
the seed of a democracy destined to grow into
monstrous proportions, and ripen into the
bloody blossom of a military despotism by
the hands of the very class of persons who
were chiefly interested in preventing it
The different stages of the battle between
plebeians and patricians, or, as we term it,
Whig and Tory, as they evolved themselves
by a social necessity from time to time, belong
to the special history of Rome, not to the general philosophy of history with which we are
here concerned.   The seed of democracy sown
at the Sacred Mount went on from one stage
of expansion to another, breaking down every
barrier of hereditary privilege between the
mass of the people and the old aristocracy,
till it ended in the *Lex Hortensia*, passed
ϳ. c. 288, which gave to all ordinances passed
by the *Comitia Tributa*—that is, the people
assembled in local tribes and voting inde-
pendently of all aristocratic check or coöper-

ation—the full validity of law. And in this progress of equalization between class and class in a community, the Muse of history sees only a special illustration of a general law that every aristocracy contending for the maintenance of exclusive privilege against natural right fights a losing battle. But the necessity of the adjustment of the opposing claims of a conservative and a progressive body in the State is a very different thing from the fashion in which the adjustment may be made, and from the consequences that may grow out of the adjustment. Here there is room for any amount of wisdom, and unfortunately also for a large amount of blundering. No man can say that the Roman constitution as it stood, after the plebeians had broken through all aristocratic barriers, was a cunningly compacted machine, or that it afforded any strong guarantee against that degeneracy into license toward which all unreined democracies naturally tend. But one thing certainly was achieved. Out of the plebeian and patrician elements of the body social, no longer arrayed in hostile attitude, but fronting one another with equal rights before the law, and adjusting their forces in a fairly-balanced equilibrium, there was formed a great political corporation, deliberative and administrative, which for independence, dignity, patriotism, and sagacity, used its authority in such a masterly style and to such world-wide issues that it has earned from Mommsen the complimentary acknowledgment of having been "the first political corporation of all times."[1] This corporation was the Roman Senate, which ruled the policy of Rome for a period of 200 years, from the passing of the Hortensian Law through a long period of African and Asiatic wars down to the civil war of Sulla and Marius, 88 B.C.— a body of which we may perhaps best easily understand the composition and the virtue if we imagine the best elements of our House of Commons and the best elements of the House of Lords merged in one Supreme Assembly of practical wisdom, to the exclusion at once of the feverish factiousness and multitudinous

---

[1] With which sentence Mr. Freeman agrees. *Comparative Politics*, Lecture iii., p. 78.

babble of the one assembly, and the brainless
obstructiveness and incurable blindness of
hereditary class interests in the other. But
there was something else in the mixed constitution of Rome besides the tried wisdom and
the great practical weight of the Senate.
What was that? There was, in the first place,
the evil of an elective kingship—for the Consul
was really an annual king under a different
name, as the President of the United States is
a quadrennial king, with greatly more power
while his kingship lasts than the Queen of
Great Britain ; and this implied an annual fit
of social fever, and the annual sowing of a
germ of faction ready to shoot into luxuriance
under the strong stimulant of the love of
power. Then, as in the natural growth of
society, a new aristocracy grew up, formed by
the addition of the wealthy plebeian families
to the old family aristocracy, and along with it a
new and numerous plebeian body, practically
though not legally excluded from the privilege
of the *optimates*, the old antagonism of patrician and plebeian would revive, and the question arose, What machinery had the legislation

of the previous centuries provided to-prevent
a collision and a rupture between the antagonistic tendencies of the democratic and oligarchic elements in the State ? The answer
is, None. The authority of the Senate, great
as it was both morally and numerically, was
antagonized by the coëqual legislative authority of the *Comitia Tributa*—an assembly as
open to any agitator for factious or revolu-
tionary purposes as a meeting of a London
mob in Hyde Park, and composed of elements
of the most motley and loose description,
ready at any moment to give the solemn sanction of a national ordinance to any act of hasty
violence or calculated party move which might
flatter the vanity or feed the craving of the
masses. But this was not all. The tribunate,
originally appointed simply for the protection
of the commonalty against the rude exercise
of patrician power, had now grown to such
formidable dimensions that the popular
tribune of the day might become the most
powerful man in the State, and only require
reëlection to constitute him into a king whose
decrees the consuls and the senators must

humiliate themselves to register. Here was a
machinery cunningly, one might think, con-
structed for the purpose of working out its
own disruption, even supposing both the popular and aristocratic elements had been
composed of average good materials. But they
were not so. In the age of the Gracchi, 133 B.C.,
the high sense of honor, the proud inheritance
of an uncorrupted patrician body, and the
shrewd sense and sobriety of a sound-hearted
yeomanry, had equally disappeared. The
aristocracy were corrupted by the wealth
which flowed in from the spoils of conquest ;
they had become lovers of power rather than
lovers of Rome ; lords of the soil, not fathers
of the people ; banded together for the narrow
interests of their own order rather than for the
general well-being of the community. The
sturdy yeomanry again, of which the mass of
the original popular assemblies had been composed, had partly dwindled away under mal-
administration of the public lands, and partly
were mixed up with motley groups of citizens
of no fixed residence, and of a town rabble
who could be induced to vote for anything by

any man who knew to win their favor by a
large distribution of Sicilian corn or the exciting luxury of gladiatorial shows ; in a word,
the *populus* had become a *plebs*, or, in our
language, the people a populace. Further-
more, let it be noted that this people or populace, tied down to meet only in Rome, as the
high seat of Government, was called upon to
deal with the administration of countries as far
apart and as diverse in character as Madrid and
Cairo, or Bagdad and Moscow are from London. Think of a mob of London artisans, on
the motion of a Henry George, or even a ration-
al Radical like Mr. Chamberlain, drummed
together to pass laws on landed property
and taxation through all that vast domain !
But so it was ; and most unfortunately also
the original fathers of the agitation which, at
the time of the Gracchi, ranged the great
rulers of the world into two hostile factions,
stabbing one another in the back and cutting
one another's throats, and plotting and coun-
ter-plotting in every conceivable style of base-
ness, after the fashion which is now being
exemplified before us in Ireland,—the authors

of this agitation were not the demagogues, but the aristocracy ; as indeed in all cases of general discontent, social fret, and illegal violence, the parties who are accused of stirring class against class are not the agitators who appear on the scene, but the maladministrators who made their appearance necessary. Man is an animal naturally inclined to obey and to take things quietly ; insurrection is too expensive an affair to be indulged in by way of recreation ; and there is no truth in the philosophy of history more certain than that whenever the multitude of the ruled rebel against their rulers, the original fault—I do not say the whole blame, for as things go on from bad to worse there may be blame and blunders on both sides—but the original fault and germinative cause of discontent and revolt unquestionably lies with the rulers. Whatever may be said about Ireland and the Scottish Highlands, there can be no doubt that in the case of Rome the original cause of the democratizing of the old constitution and the over-riding of senatorial authority by tribunician ordinances was the senators themselves, who, in direct

contravention of the public law of the State,
with that greed for more land which is the besetting sin of every aristocracy, had quartered
themselves, after the fashion of colonial squat-
ters, on the public lands, and refused to sur-
render them to the State till compelled by the
cry of popular right against might, raised by
such patriotic and self-sacrificing agitators as
the Gracchi—patriotic men who attained their
object at last by the only means in their power,
but means so drastic that, like doctor's drugs,
they drave out one devil by bringing in a score,
and paid for the partial healing of an incurable
disease by destroying forever the balance of
the constitution, and inaugurating with their
own martyr blood one of the most woful epochs
in human history—an epoch varied by period-
ical assassinations and consummated by whole-
sale butcheries.

I said the Gracchi attained their object, and
that by appointing a Commission for a distribution of the public lands, such as the friends
of the crofters in the Highlands now propose
for the repeopling of the old depopulated
homes of the clan. But I said also that the

disease under which Rome labored was incurable. How was this? Simply because, whatever might have been the merits of the special
Agrarian Law carried by the Gracchi, the violent steam by which the State machine was
moved remained the same, the clumsy machine
itself remained, and the materials with which
it had to deal in a long and critical course of
foreign cónquest became every year larger and
more unmanageable. It was not to be expected
either, on the one hand, that a strong and influential aristocracy should die with a single
kick, or, on the other, that a democracy, which
had once learned the power of a popular flood
to break down aristocratic dams, would cease
to exercise that power when a convenient occasion offered. And so the strife of oligarchic
and plebeian factions continued. The political struggle, as always happens in such cases,
became a struggle for personal supremacy ; the
sanguinary street battle between the younger
Gracchus and the Consul Opimius, though fol-
lowed by a lull for a season, was renewed after
a few years in more startling form and much ·
bloodier issues, first between Marius and Sulla,

and finally between Cæsar and Pompey. Such
a succession of embittered civil wars could end
only in exhaustion and submission ; and this
is the last emphatic lesson which the history
of Rome has taught to the governors of the
people. Every constitution of mixed aristocratic and democratic elements which fails by
kindly control on the one side, and reasonable
demand on the other, to achieve that balance
of those antagonizing forces which means good
government, must end in a military despotism.
That which will not bridle itself must be
bridled ; and when constant irritation, fretful
jars, and cruel collisions are the bloody fruit
of unchastened liberty, slavery and stagnation
seem not too high a price to pay for peace.

I have enlarged on the development and decay of the Roman republic, not only because in
point of political achievement Rome is by
far the most notable of the great States of the
world, but because in the struggle between aristocracy and democracy which was the salient
feature of its history from the expulsion of the
kings to the battle of Actium, it presents a very
close and instructive parallel to what has been

going on among ourselves from the revolution settlement of 1688 to the present hour.
If for annual kings with large power we put
hereditary kings with small power, the parallel is complete.[1] Let us now cast a glance, for
time and space allow us no more, over some
modern developments. The modern States of
Europe have good reason, upon the whole, to
think themselves fortunate in their having retained the kingship, which the Greeks and
Romans rejected, either as their original type,
or elevated and glorified from the dukedoms,
margravates, and electorates with which they
started. There cannot be much doubt, I imagine, that, if the Romans had retained their
king in a hereditary or nearly hereditary form,
he might have exercised a mediatorial function
between the contending parties that would
have prevented those bloody strifes and those
ugly civic wounds with which the record of
their political career stands now so sorrowfully
defaced. In the experience of their own earliest story, Servius Tullius had already shown

[1] This parallel has been noticed by the thoughtful Germans;
see particularly Zacharia Sulla, i. 40.

them how a king in the strife of classes might
step in by a peaceful new model to open the
ranks of a close aristocracy with dignity and
safety to a rising democracy; and in modern
times the case of Leopold II. of Tuscany does
not stand alone as an example of what good
service a wise king may do in the adjustment
of contending claims and smoothing the march
of necessary social transitions. In fact, the
most democratic people among the ancients,
in order to effect such an adjustment in a peaceful way, had been obliged to make Solon a
king for the nonce; and the Romans, urged
by a like social pressure, named their dictator,
or reëlected their consuls and their tribunes,
in order to secure for the need of the moment
that unity of counsel, energy of conduct, and
moral authority which is the grand recom-
mendation of the kingship. No doubt kings
in modern as in ancient times have erred; they
have not been able always to keep themselves
sober under the intoxicating influence of absolute power, and they have paid dearly for
their errors; but we were wise in this country,
while beheading one despot and banishing

another, to punish the offender without abolishing the office. True, a thorough-going and
sternly-consistent republican may ask, with
an indignant sneer, What is the use of a king,
when we have shorn him of all honors save the
grace of a crown and the bauble of a sceptre—
reduced him, in fact, to a mere machine to
register the decrees of a democratic assembly?
But such persons require to be reminded that
there is nothing more dangerous, not only in
political, but in all practical matters, than
logical consistency; that the most narrow-
minded people are always the most consistent,
and this for the very obvious reason that they
have only room for one idea in their small
brain chambers, whereas God's world contains
many ideas, stiff ideas too, and given to battle,
which must be brought into some friendly balance or compromise, or set about throat-cut-
ting on a large scale—a process to which consistent republicans have never shown a less
bloody inclination than consistent monarchists.
They must be reminded also that the person
of the monarch is an incarnated, visible, and
tangible symbol of the unity of the nation, of

which parties and factions are so apt to be forgetful ; and if our logically-consistent republican may look on this as a matter of association and sentiment which he will not acknowledge, he must simply be told that the man who does not acknowledge the important place played by associations and sentiments in all matters of Church and State knows nothing of human nature, and is altogether unfit for meddling with the difficult and dangerous art of politics. He may write books, and lecture to coteries, and harangue electoral meetings, and delight himself largely in the reverberation of his own wisdom, but by all means let him not be a prime minister. To what ends logical consistency can lead a politician in high places Charles I. and Archbishop Laud learned when it was too late ; and the fate of these two high-perched worthies stands as a speaking lesson to all politicians, whether of the democratic or the monarchical type, how easy a thing it is for a man to be a good Christian and a consistent thinker, and yet on all political matters a perfect fool.

Among the notable modern States three

stand before us with an exceptional prefer-
ence for the democratic form of government—
Switzerland, France, and the great trans-At-
lantic Republic. These must be regarded
with curious interest and kindly human sympathy as great social experiments, by no means
to be prejudged and denounced by any sweeping conclusions made from the unfortunate
breakdown of the two celebrated ancient re-
publics. The experiment in these cases, as
made in altogether different circumstances and
under different conditions, cannot warrant
any such denunciations. The representative
system which now universally prevails, and
which enables a most widely-scattered and
diverse - minded population to vote with a
coolness and a precision and a large survey
of which the urban system of Greece and
Rome never dreamed; the general growth of
intelligence among all classes through the action of cheap education and the large circulation of cheap books; the rapid and ever more
rapid travelling of contagious thought from
the centre to the extreme limbs and flourishes
of social unities; and, above all, let us hope

the improved tone of social feeling in all the
relations of man to man, which we owe to the
great Christian principle of living as brother
with brother, and sister with sister, under a
common heavenly fatherhood,—these are all
forces largely operating in the present day
which justify us in hoping that many a social
experiment which signally failed with the ancients may be crowned in the centuries which
are now being inaugurated with encouraging
success. Of the three which we have named,
Switzerland is the country in which, from
topographical peculiarities, the interests of
jealous neighbors, and the traditional habits
of a peasant population well trained to provincial self-government, the permanence of a
democratic federation may be prophesied with
the greatest safety, but at the same time with
the least interest to the general march of
humanity. Ancient Rome, had it continued
as compact and as little disturbed by external
forces and internal fermentations as modern
Switzerland, might have remained during the
whole course of its career as sober-minded and
as stable as in the days of Cincinnatus, and

the yeomanry which were displaced by huge
absentee landlords, and Syrian or Sicilian
slaves. The case of France is altogether different. A republic in an over-civilized, highly-
centralized, bureaucratically-governed country, with a religiously hollow, hasty, violent,
excitable, and explosive people, seems of all
social experiments the least hopeful : and that
is all that can wisely be said of it at present.
But the social conditions in America are altogether different ; and the experiment of a great
democratic republic for the first time in the
history of the world—for Rome in its best
times, as we have seen, was an aristocracy—
will be looked on by all lovers of their species
with the most kindly curiosity and the most
hopeful sympathy. Here we have the stout,
self-reliant, sober-minded Anglo-Saxon stock,
well trained in the process of the ages to the
difficult art of self-government ; here we have
a constitution framed with the most cautious
consideration, and with the most effective
checks against the dangers of an over-riding
democracy ; here also a people as free from
any imminent external danger as they have

unlimited scope for internal progress. Under
no circumstances could the experiment of self-
government, on a great scale, have been made
with a more promising start. No doubt they
have a difficult and slippery problem to perform. The frequent recurrence of elections to
the supreme magistracy has always been, and
ever must be, the breeder of faction, the nurse
of venality, and the spur of ambition. Once
already has this Titanic confederacy, though
only a hundred years old, by going through a
process of a long, bitter, and bloody civil
war, shown that the unifying machinery so
cunningly put together by the conservative
genius of a Washington, an Adams, and a
Madison, was insufficient to hold in check the
rebellious forces at war within its womb. No
doubt also it were in vain to speak America
free from those acts of gigantic jobbing, blushless venality, and over-riding of the masses in
various ways, which were working the ruin of
Rome in the days of Jugurtha. The aristocracy of gold and the tyranny of capitalists in
Christian New York has shown itself no less
able to usurp the public land and defraud the

people of their share in the soil than the lordly
aristocracy and the slave-dealing magnates of
heathen Rome. Nevertheless we need not
despair. The sins of American democracy
may serve as a useful hint to us not rashly to
tinker our own mixed constitution without
waiting for a verdict on issues, which, as
Socrates wisely says, lie with the gods; nor,
on the other hand, is there any wisdom in
ascribing to the American form of government evils which, as belonging to human
nature, crop up with more or less abundance
under all forms of government, and which
may be specially rife among ourselves. We
also have our Glasgow banks, our bubble
companies of all kinds, our heady speculations, our hot competitions, our over-produc-
tions, our haste to be rich, our idol worship
of mere material magnificence,— these are
evils, and the root of all evil, with the production of which no form of government has
anything to do, and against which every form
of government will be in vain invoked to
contend.

In conclusion, we must bear in mind that

democracy or social self-government is the
most difficult of all human problems, and
must be approached, not with inflated hopes
and rosy imaginations, but with sobriety and
caution and a sound mind, and at critical
moments not without prayer and fasting.
Before entering on any scheme for rebuilding
our social edifice on a democratic model, we
should consider seriously what a democracy
really implies, and what we may reasonably
promise ourselves from its possible success.
Of the two rallying cries which have made it
a favorite with persons given to change, equality and liberty, the one is no more true than
that all the mountains in the Highlands are as
high as Ben Nevis, and can only mean at the
best that all men have an equal right to be called
men and to be treated as men, while the other
is only true so far as concerns the removal of
all artificial barriers to the free exercise of
each man's function, according to his capacity
and opportunities. But this is a mere starting-
point in the social life of a great people. When
the bird is out of the cage, which it must be in
order to be a perfect bird, the more serious

question emerges, what use it shall make of
its newly-acquired liberty. Here certainly to
men, as to birds, there are great dangers to be
faced ; and with nations the progress of society,
as already remarked, is measured to a much
larger extent by the increase of limitations
than by the extension of liberties. Then,
again, the fundamental postulate of extreme
democracy that the majority have everywhere
a right to govern is manifestly false. No man
as a member of society has a natural right to
govern : he has a right to be governed, and
well governed ; and that can only be when the
government is conducted by the wisest and
best men who compose the society. If the
numerical majority is composed of sober-
minded, sensible, and intelligent persons who
will either govern wisely themselves or choose
persons who will do so, then democracy is
justified by its deeds ; but if it is otherwise,
and if, when an appeal is made to the multitude, they will choose the most daring, the
most ambitious, and the most unscrupulous,
rather than the most sensible, the most moderate, and the most conscientious, then democ-

racy is a bad thing, at least nothing better
than the other *ocracies* which it supplants. It
is manifest, therefore, that of all forms of government democracy is that which imperatively
requires the greatest amount of intelligence
and moderation among the great mass of the
people, especially among the lower classes,
who have always been the most numerous;
and, as history can point to no quarter of the
world where such a happy condition of the
numerical intelligence has been realized, it
cannot look with any favor on schemes of universal suffrage, even when qualified with a
stout array of effective checks. The system,
indeed, of representing every man individually,
and giving every member of a society a capitation vote, as they have a capitation tax in
Turkey, however popular with the advocates
of extreme democracy, seems quite unreasona-
ble. What requires to be represented in a
reasonable representative system is not so
much individuals as qualities, capacities, interests, and types. Every class should be
represented, rather than every man in a class.
Besides, the equality of votes which democracy

demands, on the principle that I am as good
as you and perhaps a little better, is utterly
false, and tends to nourish conceit and imper-
tinence, to banish all reverence, and to ignore
all distinctions in society. Anyhow, there
can be no doubt that great masses of men
acting together on exciting occasions are
peculiarly liable to hasty resolutions and violent opinions ; all democracies, therefore, are
. unsafe which are unprovided with checks in
the form of an upper chamber composed of
more cool materials, and planted firmly in a
position that makes them independent of the
fever and faction of the hour. A strong democracy stands as much in need of an aristocratic rein as a strong aristocracy does of a
democratic spur. And let it never be forgotten—what democracies are far too apt to forget—that minorities have rights as well as
majorities ; nay, that one of the great ends to
be achieved by a good government is to pro-
tect the few against the natural insolence of a
majority glorying in its numbers, and hurried on by the spring-tide of a popular con-
tagion. A state of society is not at all incon-

ceivable in which the many shall make all the laws and monopolize all the offices of a fussy bureaucracy, while the few are burdened with all the taxes. Never too frequently can we repeat, in reference to all public acts, no less than to the conduct of individuals in private life, the great Aristotelian maxim that ALL EXTREMES ARE WRONG ; that every force when in full action tends to an excess which for its own salvation must be met by a counterpoising force ; that all good government, as all healthy existence, is the balance of opposites and the marriage of contraries ; and that the more mettlesome the charger the more need of a firm rein and a cautious rider. He who overlooks this prime postulate of all sane action in this complex world may pile his democratic house tier above tier and enjoy his green conceit for a season ; but the day of sore trial and civic storm is not far, when the rain shall descend, and the floods come, and the winds blow and beat upon that house, and it will fall, because it was founded upon a dream.

THE CHURCH.

II.

THE CHURCH.

Οὐ πᾶς ὁ λέγων μοι Κύριε, Κύριε, εἰσελεύσεται εἰς τὴν βασιλείαν τῶν οὐρανῶν· ἀλλ' ὁ ποιῶν τὸ θέλημα τοῦ πατρός μου τοῦ ἐν τοῖς οὐρανοῖς.—Ὁ ΣΩΤΗΡ.

MAN is characteristically a religious animal; in fact, as Socrates teaches, the only religious animal;[1] for, though a dog has no doubt reverential emotions, it cannot be said with any propriety that he has religious ideas or ecclesiastical institutions, for a very good reason, because he has no ideas at all : observation he has very keen, and memory also wonderfully retentive; instincts also, like all primal vital forces, divine and miraculous; but ideas certainly none, for ideas mean knowledge; and brutes that have no language properly so called,

---

[1] τίνος γὰρ ἄλλου ζῴου ψυχὴ πρῶτα μὲν θεῶν τῶν τὰ μέγιστα καὶ κάλλιστα συνταξάντων ᾔσθηται ὅτι εἰσὶ : τί δὲ φῦλον ἄλλο ἢ ἄνθρωποι θεοὺς θεραπεύουσι. —Xen. *Mem.* i. 4.

that is a system of significant vocal signs expressive of ideas, but only cries, gesticulations, and visible or audible signs expressive of sensations and feelings, can by no law of natural analogy be credited with the possession of a faculty of which they give no manifestation. Language is the outward body and form of which thought and reason and knowledge and ideas are the inward soul and force; and hence the wise Greeks, unlike our modern scientists, who delight in confounding man with the monkey, expressed language and reason with one word λόγος, while what we dignify with the name of language in birds and other animals was simply φωνή, or significant voice. If, therefore, there is any thing most human that history has to teach, it must be about religion. All the great nations whose names mark the march of human fates have been religious nations. A people without religion does not exist, or, if it does exist, it exists only as an abnormal and deficient specimen of the genus to which it belongs, which is of no more account in the just estimate of the type than a fox without a tail, or a lawyer

without a tongue ; and as for individual athe-
ists, who have been talked about in ancient
times, and specially in these latter days, they
are either philosophers like Spinoza, the most
pious of men, falsely baptized with an odious
title from the stupidity, prejudice, or malice
of the community, or, if they really are athe-
ists, they are monsters which a man may stare
at as at an ass with three heads or with no head
at all in a show.

The form in which religion generally presents itself in early history is what we commonly call Polytheism, though it is quite
possible—a matter about which I am not careful curiously to dogmatize—that there may
have been in some places an original Dualism,
like the ancient Persian, or even a Monothe-
ism, out of which the Polytheism was developed.   For there cannot be the slightest doubt
that, whatever may have been the starting-
point, there lay in the popular theology a
tendency to multiply and to reproduce itself
in kindred but not always easily recognizable
forms, like the children of a family or the
cousinship of a clan.   But, taking Polytheism

as the type under which history presents the
objects of religious faith in the earliest times,
we have to remark that under this common
name, as in the case of Christianity, the greatest contrasts, both in speculative idea and in
social efficiency, stare us everywhere in the
face. In the eye of the Christian or the monotheistic devotee the worships of Aphrodite and
of Pallas Athene are equally idolatrous ; but,
allowing that these anthropomorphic forms of
divine forces and functions of the universe are
equally destitute of a foundation in fact or
reason, the reverence paid to them by a devout
people might be as different as passion is from
thought, and sense from spirit. As the ideal
of wisdom in counsel and in action, the Athenian Pallas no doubt exercised as beneficent a
sway over her Hellenic worshippers as the
ideal of Christian womanhood, in the person
of the Virgin Mary, does at the present day
over millions of Christian worshippers. It is
only when the cosmic function impersonated
in the polytheistic god, being of an inferior
order, leaps from its proper position of subordination and usurps the controlling and regu-

lating action belonging to the superior function, that polytheistic idolatry becomes immoral; though, of course, the very facility of this usurpation, and the stamp of a pseudo divinity that may thereby be given to beastly vice, is a sufficient reason for the denunciations of the heathen idolatries so frequent in the Old Testament, which ultimately ripened into the spiritual apostleship and monotheistic aggression of St. Paul. One other striking feature of all polytheistic religions may not be omitted. They are naturally complete—more catholic, more sympathetic with universal nature and universal life than monotheistic religions; if they make a philosophical mistake in worshipping many gods, they do not make a moral mistake in excluding any of his attributes. With the polytheistic worshipper everything is sacred: the sun and the sea and the sky, dark earth and awful night, excite in him an emotion of reverence. If the Greek polytheist was devout at all, he was devout everywhere; whereas, under monotheistic influences, there is a danger that devout feelings may respond exclusively to the stern decrees of an absolute

lawgiver and the awful threatenings of a vio-
lated law.   Polytheistic piety, whatever its
defects, was always ready to add a grace to
every innocent enjoyment ; monotheistic relig-
iousness, as we see its severe features in some
modern churches, contents itself with adding
a solemn sanction to the moral law—a severity
which here and there has not been able to keep
itself free from the unlovely phase of regard-
ing the innocent enjoyments and the graceful
pleasantries of life as a sin.

So much for the soul of the business; the
body is what we call the Church.   And here
the very word is significant.   In one sense, as
a separate ethical corporation, the ancients
had no Church.   Why ?   Because Church and
State were one ; or, if they were two, they
were two like the famous Siamese twins that
used to be carried about the country as a show,
two so closely connected that they could no
more be torn from one another and live than
the limpet can be separated from the rock to
which it clings.   With the peoples of the ancient world the State was the Church and the
Church was the State ; the priest was a

magistrate and the magistrate was a priest.
This identity of two things, or loose intercom-
munion and fusion of two things in modern
association so instinctively kept apart, arose
from the common germ out of which both
Church and State grew—viz., as we saw in the
previous lecture, the FAMILY. Every father
of a family, in the normal and healthy state of
society, is his own priest as well as his own
king. In religion and morals, as well as in all
domestic ordinances, he is absolute and supreme; and the functions which necessarily
belonged to him as supreme administrator in
his own family would, under the influence of
family feelings, naturally be conceded to him
when the family grew to a clan, and the clan
to a kingdom. And this is the state of things
which we meet with in the Book of Genesis,
long before the promulgation of the Mosaic
law, where we read (xiv. 18) that Melchizedek,
king of Salem, went out to bless Abraham, and
he was *priest* of the Most High God ; the distinction between priest and layman, to which
our ears are so familiar, being in this, as in
a thousand other well-known instances, alto-

gether ignored. Not only in Homer, where we find Agamemnon, the king of men, performing sacrificial functions without even the presence of a priest,[1] but in the sober historical age we find the King of Sparta performing all the public sacrifices—being, in fact, in virtue of his office, high priest of Jove.[2] So closely indeed was the State religion identified with the person of the supreme magistrate that, when the kingship was abolished in Greece, and three principal archons and seven secondary ones shared his functions, one still retained the title of βασιλεύς, *king*, and had the supervision, or, as we would say, supreme episcopacy and overseership of all matters pertaining to religion.[3] The same thing took place in Rome, where the name of king was even more odious than in Greece; but nevertheless a *rex sacrificulus*, or *king-sacrificer*, with his *regina* or *queen*, took rank in all the public pontifical dinners above the *pontifex maximus* himself. The college of pontiffs in

---

[1] *Iliad*, iii. 271 ; and compare Virgil, *Æneid*, iii. 80.
[2] Xen., *Rep. Lac.*, i. 15 ; Herod. vi. 56.
[3] Pollux, viii. 90.

Rome, which had the supreme direction of all
religious matters, was not a board of priests,
but of laymen—or at least of laymen who,
without any qualification but some inaugurating ceremony, might be assumed into the
pontifical college ; whence the title of *pontifex
maximus*, which the emperors assumed, was
no more of the nature of a usurpation than the
title of *imperator*, which belonged to them as
supreme commanders of the army. Who, then,
were the priests, and what need of them at all
if the laity might legally perform all their
functions? The answer is simple. Both in
Greece and Rome there were priests and
priestly families, as the *Eumolpidæ* in Eleusis,
specially dedicated to the service of certain
local gods ; but there was no order, class, or
body of persons having the exclusive right to
officiate in sacred matters over the whole community. No doubt the social position of priests
in democratic Greece and monarchical Egypt
was extremely different, but in one respect.
they were identical : in Athens Church and
State were one as much as in Memphis. In
Egypt there was a remarkably strong body or

clan of priests enjoying the highest dignities
and immunities ; but there is no proof'that
they were a caste, in the strict sense of the
word ; and their virtues were so far from being incommunicable that, when the Pharaoh
did not happen to be a born priest, but of the
military class, he was obliged to be made a
priest before he could be a king; and when
once king he became *ipso facto* the high
priest of the nation, and took precedence of
all priests in all great public acts of religious
ceremonial. It must not be supposed, however, that, though he was supreme in all
sacred matters and the actual head of the
Church, to use our language, he could set
himself, like our Henry VIII., to carve creeds
for the people, and imprison or burn devout
persons for refusing to acknowledge his arbitrary decrees. The exercise of sacred functions in the hands of the masterful Tudor and
his Machiavelian minister was a usurpation
tolerated by a loyal people as their readiest
and most effective way of getting rid of the
masterdom of the Roman Pope, which in
those days pressed like an incubus on the

European conscience; it was invoking one
devil to turn out another, and was successful,
as such operations are wont to be, in a blundering sort of way. But the worshipful
" Sons of the Sun "—for so they were betitled
—on the banks of the sweet-watered Nile, had
no monstrous pretension of this kind, and
could not even have dreamt of it. They did
not sit on the throne to reform religion, but to
maintain it. Neither in Egypt nor in Greece
in those days was any such thing known as
the rights of the individual conscience; but
both kings and people received religious laws
and consuetudes as we do *Magna Charta;*
reasonable people, in the long course of the
centuries before Christ, would no more dream
of disturbing the ancestral belief about the
gods than they would think of influencing
the settled courses of the stars. It was their
very deep-rooted permanency, in the midst of
the startling mutabilities to which human
affairs are liable, that made the fundamental
truths of religion so valuable to their souls;
and as to the particular forms under which
these fundamental truths might have been

symbolized by venerable tradition, the people were not given to form themselves into hostile camps on the ground of any local difference, as we do in Scotland about ecclesiastical conceits and crotchets ; and every devout Egyptian allowed his neighbor without offence to pay sacred honors to a crocodile or a cat, convinced that these honors were equally legitimate and equally beneficial whenever the sacred symbolism peculiar to the worship was wisely understood. Collisions, therefore, between Church and State, or between priesthood and kingship, such as signalized the medieval struggles of the Popes and Emperors, and the convulsions of our infant Protestant freedom in England, could not take place among the ancient polytheists. A wise Socrates was equally willing with the most superstitious devotee, when pious gratitude called, to sacrifice a cock to Æsculapius ; and the νόμῳ πόλεως, by the custom of the State, was the direction which he gave to all who inquired of him by what rites they ought to worship the gods.[1] Only among the He-

---

[1] Xen., *Mem.* i. 3.

brews, as a people in whose religious habitude
polytheistic and monotheistic tendencies had
never come to any decisive settlement of their
inherent antagonism, do I find a record of a
very serious collision between Church and
State, after the fashion of our German Henries
and Transalpine Hildebrands in the days of
Papal aggression. Scotsmen familiar with
their Bibles will easily see that I allude to
the case of Uzziah, as recorded in 2 Chron.
xxvi. 16-20 :—"But when he was strong, his
heart was lifted up to his destruction : for he
transgressed against the Lord his God, and
went into the temple of the Lord to burn
incense upon the altar of incense. And Azariah
the priest went in after him, and with him
fourscore priests of the Lord, that were valiant
men : And they withstood Uzziah the king,
and said unto him, It appertaineth not unto
thee, Uzziah, to burn incense unto the Lord,
but to the priests the sons of Aaron, that are
consecrated to burn incense : go out of the
sanctuary ; for thou hast trespassed ; neither
shall it be for thine honor from the Lord God.
Then Uzziah was wroth, and had a censer in

his hand to burn incense: and while he was wroth with the priests, the leprosy even rose up in his forehead before the priests in the house of the Lord, from beside the incense altar. And Azariah the chief priest, and all the priests, looked upon him, and, behold, he was leprous in his forehead, and they thrust him out from thence; yea, himself hasted also to go out, because the Lord had smitten him."

So much for Polytheism. That it should have served the spiritual needs of the human heart so long—five thousand years at least, from the first Pharaoh that looked down from his Memphian pyramid on the mystic form of the Sphinx, to the last Roman Emperor that sacrificed white bulls from Clitumnus at the altar of the Capitoline Jove—is proof sufficient that, with all its faults, it was made of very serviceable stuff; but creeds and kingdoms, like individuals, must die. At the commencement of the eighth century of the Roman Republic heathenism was doomed in all Romanized Europe, in all Northern Africa, and in Western Asia, and that for four reasons. The polytheistic religions of the Old World, cre-

ated as they were in the infancy of society, no
doubt under the guidance of a healthy instinct
of dependence on the ruling power of the
universe, but in the main inspired by the
emotions and formulated by the imagination,
without the regulating control of reason, could
not hope to hold their ground permanently in
the face of that rich growth of individual
speculation which, from the sixth century
before Christ, spread with such ample ramifi-
cation from Asiatic and European Greece over
the greater part of the civilized world. If it
was a necessity of human beings at all times
to have a religion, it was a no less urgent
problem, as the range of vision enlarged with
the process of the ages, to harmonize their
theology with their thinking. And if, on the
intellectual side, the polytheistic religions of
that cultivated age were threatened with a
collapse, the sensuous element, always strongly
represented in emotional faiths, was in constant danger of being dragged down into a
disturbing and degrading sensuality. Then,
again, when the Roman Republic, in the age
of Augustus Cæsar, had completed the range

of its world-wide conquests, two social forces, unknown in the best ages of Greece and Rome, viz., wealth and luxury, added their perilous momentum to the corrupting elements which were already at work in the bosom of the polytheistic system. And in what a hot-bed of fermenting putridity these evil leavens had resulted at this period, the pages of Suetonius and many chapters in St. Paul are witnesses equally credible and equally tragic. Add to all this the fact that the motley intermixture of ideas and the inorganic confusion and forced assimilation of creeds which accompanied the universal march of Roman polity brought about a vague desire for some sort of religious unity which might run parallel with the political unity under which men lived ; and this desire could be gratified only by placing in the foreground the great truth of the unity of the Supreme Being, which to vindicate in pre-Christian ages had been the special mission of the Hebrew race, and which the Greeks themselves had not indistinctly indicated by placing the moral government of the world and the issues of peace and war in

the hands of an omnipotent, all-wise, all-benef-
icent, and absolute Jove. These and the like
considerations will lead the thoughtful student
of history easily to understand how the appearance of such an extraordinary moral force
as Christianity was imperatively called for at
the period when our Saviour, with His divine
mission to a fallen race, began His preaching
on the shores of a lonely Galilean lake ; and
the most superficial glance at the contents of
His preaching, as contrasted with the heathenism which it replaced, will show how wonder-
ful was the new start which it gave to the
moral life of the world, and how effective the
spur which it applied to the march of the ages
—a spur so potent that we may, without the
slightest exaggeration, say that to Christianity we owe almost exclusively whatever mild
agencies tempered the harshness and sweet-
ened the sourness of crude government in the
Middle Ages ; and no less, whatever hopeful
elements are at the present moment working
among ourselves to save the British people, at
a critical stage of their social development,
from the decadence and the degradation that

overtook the Romans after their great military
mission had been fulfilled. Let us look artic-
ulately at the main constituents of that new
leaven wherewith Christianity was equipped
to regenerate the world. These I find to be—

(1.) By asserting in the strongest way the
unity of God, it at once cut the root of the
tendency in human nature to create arbitrary
objects of worship according to the lust or
fancy of the worshipper, and accustomed the
popular intelligence to a harmonized view of
the various forces at work in the constitution
of a world so various and so complex as to a
superficial view readily to appear contradictory
and irreconcilable.

(2.) By preaching the unity of God, not as
an abstract metaphysical idea, but as what it
really is, a divine fatherhood, Christianity at
one stroke bound all men together as brethren
and members of a common family ; and in this
way, while in the relation of nation to nation
it substituted apostleships of love for wars of
subjugation, in the relation of class to class it
established a sort of spiritual democracy, in
which the implied equality of all men as men

gradually led to the abolition of the abnormal institution of slavery, on which all ancient society rested.

(3.) Christianity, by starting religion as an independent moral association altogether separate from the State, at once purified the sphere of the Church from corrupting elements, and confined the State within those bounds which the nature of a civic administration furnishes. Religion in this way was purified and elevated, because in its nicely segregated sphere no secular considerations of any kind could interfere to tone down its ideal, direct its current, or lame its efficiency ; while the State, on the other hand, was saved from the folly of intermeddling with matters which it did not understand, and professing principles which it did not believe.

(4.) Christianity, by planting itself emphatically at the very first start, as one may see in the Sermon on the Mount, in direct antagonism to ritualism, ceremonialism, and every variety of externalism, and placing the essence of all true religion in regeneration, or, as St. Paul has it, a new creature—i. e. the legitimate practical dominance of the spiritual and ethical above the sensual and carnal part of our nature—broke down the middle wall of partition which had so often divided piety from morality ; so that now a man of culture might consistently give his right hand to religion and his left hand to philosophy, an attitude which, so long as Homer was all that the Greeks had for a bible, no devout Hellenist could assume.

(5.) By placing a firm belief in a future life as a guiding prospect in the foreground, the religion of Christ gave the highest possible value to human life, and the strongest possible spur to perseverance in a virtuous career.

(6.) By appealing directly to the individual conscience, and making religion a matter of personal concern and of moral conviction, it raised the value of each individual as a responsible moral agent, and placed the dignity of every man as a social monad on the firmest possible pedestal.

(7.) By making love its chief motive power, it supplied both the steam and the oil of the social machine with a continuity of moral force never dreamt of in any of the ancient societies

—a force which no mere socialistic schemes for
organizing labor, no boards of health, no political economy, no mathematical abstractions,
no curiosities of physical science, no democratic suffrages, and no school inspectorships,
though multiplied a thousand times, apart from
this divine agency, can ever hope to achieve.

Thus equipped with a moral armature such
as the world had never yet seen, it might have
been expected that the triumph of Christianity
over the ruins of heathenism would have been
as complete and as pure from all admixture of
evil as it appears in the great evangelical
manifesto commonly called the Sermon on the
Mount. But it was not to be so ; nor, indeed,
created as human nature is, could possibly be.
The miraculous virtue of the seed could not
change the nature of the soil, and the sweet
new wine put into old bottles could not fail to
catch a taint from the acid incrustations of the
original liquor. *Corruptia optimi pessima* is
the great lesson which history everywhere
teaches, and nowhere with a more tragic im-
pressiveness than in the history of the Christian Church. What a rank crop of old wives'

fables, endless genealogies, ceremonial observances, worship of the letter, voluntary humili-
ties, and disputations of science, falsely so
called, started into fretful array before the
spiritual swordsmanship of St. Paul, no reader
of the grandest correspondence in the world
need be told ; but it was not so much from
Jewish drivel, Attic subtlety, or Corinthian
sensualism, that the corrupting forces were to
proceed which in the post-Apostolic age in-
sinuated themselves like a poison into the pure
blood of the Church. It is from within that,
in moral matters, our great danger flows : if
the kingdom of heaven is there, the kingdom
of hell is there no less distinctly. The doctrine
of Aristotle, and the teaching of history that
ALL EXTREMES ARE WRONG, is ever and ever
repeated to passion-spurred mortals, and ever
and ever forgotten. In the green ardor of our
worship we make an idol of our virtue ; the
strong lines of the particular excellence which
we admire are stretched into a caricature ; our
sublime, severed from all root of soundness,
reels over into the ridiculous ; we revel and
riot and get into an intoxicated excitement

with the fruit of our own fancy ; and work
ourselves from one stage of inflammation to
another, till, as our great dramatist says,

"Goodness, grown to a pleurisy,
Dies of its own too much."

The excess into which Christianity at its first
start most naturally fell was ultra-spiritualism,
asceticism, or by whatever name we may
choose to characterize that high-flying system
in morals which, not content with the regulation and subordination, aims at the violent
subjugation and, as much as may be, the total
suppression of the physical element in man.
How near this abuse lay is evident, not only
from the general tendency of every man to
make an idol of his distinctive virtue, and of
every sect to delight in the exaggeration of its
most characteristic feature, but there are not a
few passages of the New Testament which
plainly show that the masculine Christianity
of St. Paul had not more occasion to protest
against those Greek libertines who turned the
grace of God into licentiousness, than against
those offshoots of the Jewish Essenes who pro-
fessed a self-imposed arbitrary religiosity (Col.

ii. 18, 23), even forbidding to marry and commanding to abstain from meats (1 Tim. iv. 3).[1] There is indeed, something very seductive in these attempts to acquire a superhuman virtue, whether they be made by a poet casting off the vulgar bonds that bind him to his fellows, like Percy Bysshe Shelley, that he may feed upon sun-dews and get drunk on transcendental imaginations, or by a religious person, that he may devote himself to spiritual exercises, free from the disturbing influence of earthly passions. Such a renunciation of the flesh gratifies his pride, and has, in fact, the aspect of a heroic virtue in a special line ; while, at the same time, it is with some persons more convenient, inasmuch as when the resolution is once formed and a decided start made, it is always easier to abstain than to be moderate. Nevertheless, all such ambitious schemes to ignore the body and to cut short the natural rights of our physical nature must

---

[1] From the διδαχή τῶν ἀποστόλων, or *Early Teaching of the Apostles,* lately discovered, ch. viii., we learn that it was the custom of the early Christians to observe two days of fasting in the week—Wednesday and Friday.—Edit. Oxford Parker, 1885.

fail. It never can be the virtue of a man to wish to be more than man ; and every religion which sets a stamp of special approval on superhuman, and therefore unhuman, virtue, erects a wall of separation between the gospel which it preaches and the world which it should convert. In fact, it rather gives up the world in despair, and institutes an artificial school for the practice of certain select virtues, which only a few will practice, and which, when practiced, can only make those few unfit for the social position which Providence meant them to occupy.

The second excess into which Christianity, under the action of frail human nature, easily ran was intolerance. This intolerance, as in the previous case, is only a virtue run to seed ; for, as all asceticism is merely a misapplication or an exaggeration of the virtue of self-denial and self-control, so all intolerance, or defect of kindly regard to the contrary in opinion or conduct, is merely a crude or an impolitic extension of the imperative OUGHT which lies at the root of all moral truth, and specially of all monotheistic religions. There

is, indeed, a certain intolerance in truth which
will not allow it to hold parley with error;
and every new religion with a lofty inspiration, conscious of a divine mission, is necessarily aggressive: it delights to pluck the
beard of ancestral authority, and marches
right into the presence of hoary absurdity and
consecrated stupidity.   No doubt there is a
boundary here which the divine wisdom of
the Son of God pointed at emphatically enough
when he was asked to bring down fire from
heaven on those who taught or did otherwise ;
but the evil spirit of self-importance which
prompted this request was too deeply en-
grained in human nature to be eradicated by a
single warning of the great teacher.   This
spirit of arrogant individualism asserted itself
at an early period in the disorderly Corinthian
Church very much in the same way as it does
among ourselves, specially in Scotland, at
the present moment—viz. by the multiplication of sects, the exaggeration of petty distinctions, and the fomenting of petty rivalries,—
" Now this I say, that every one of you saith,
I am of Paul ; and I of Apollos ; and I of Ce-

phas; and I of Christ" (1 Cor. i. 12),—a spirit
which the apostle most strongly denounces as
proceeding manifestly from the overrated
importance of some secondary specialty, or
some accessory condition, of the body of believers, who thus clubbed themselves into a
denomination, and resulting in an unkindly
divergence from the common highway of evangelic life, and an intolerant desire to over-
ride one Christian brother with the private
shibboleth of another, and to stamp him with
the seal of their own conceit. The field in
which this intolerant spirit displayed itself
was of course different, according to the influences at work at the time; but there is one
field which, if church history is to teach us
anything, we are bound to emphasize strongly,
that is the field of dogma; for, if there be any
influence that has worked more powerfully to
discredit Christianity than even the immoral
lives and selfish maxims of professing Christians, it is the fixation and glorification and
idol-worship of the dogma. No doubt Christianity is far from being that system, or rather
no system, of vague and cloudy sentiment to

which some persons would reduce it : it has
bones, and a firm framework ; it stands upon
facts, and is not without doctrines, but it does
not make a parade of doctrines ; and the faith
which it enjoins, as is manifest from the defi-
nition and historical examples in Hebrews xi.,
is not an intellectual faith in the doctrines of
a metaphysical theology, but a living faith in
the moral government of the world and a
heroic conduct in life, as the necessary expression of such faith. The mere intellectual
orthodoxy on which the Christian Church has,
by the tradition of centuries, placed such a
high value, is, in the apostolical estimate,
plainly worth nothing ; for the devils also believe and tremble, as St. James has it, or as our
Lord himself said in the striking summation
to the Sermon on the Mount, " Not they who
call me *Lord, Lord*, shall enter into the kingdom, but they who do the will of my Father
who is in heaven. By their works, not by
their creed, ye shall know them."[1] Never-

---

[1] In the διδαχή τῶν ἀποστόλων there is absolutely no
dogma. It is all practice, end this is quite in harmony with the
use of διδαχή by St. Paul (1 Tim. i. 10), and indeed with the
whole tone of these two admirable epistles.

theless, the exaltation of the dogma has always
been a favorite tendency of the Church, and
the besetting sin of the clergy. With the
mass of the people, to swear to a curious
creed is always more easy than to lead a noble
life ; while to the clerical intellect it must
always give a secret satisfaction to think that
the science of theology, which is the furthest
removed from the handling of the great mass
of men, has in their hands assumed a well-de-
fined shape, of which the articulations are as
subtle and as necessary as the steps of solution in a difficult algebraic problem. The late
Baron Bunsen, for many years Prussian am-
bassador in London, one of the most large-
minded and large-hearted of Christian men, in
the preface to his great *Bibel werk*, devotes a
special chapter to Dogmatism as a vice of the
clerical mind leading to false views of Scripture ; over and above what he calls the modern
revival of scholastic theology in Germany, he
enumerates four dominant epochs of ecclesiastical life in which this anti-evangelical tendency has prominently asserted itself. These
are—(1) the dogmatism of the great Church

councils in the reigns of Constantine, Theodo-
sius, and Justinian ; (2) the medieval scholasticism of the Western Church; (3) the Protestant scholasticism of the sixteenth and seven-
teenth centuries ; (4) the dogmatism of the
Jesuits, Perron, Bossuet, and others. Had
this dogmatic tendency of the Church contented itself with tabulating a curious scheme of
divine mysteries, though it might justly have
been deemed impertinent, and here and there
a little presumptuous, yet it might have been
condoned lightly as a sort of clerical recreation in hours which might have been worse
employed ; but it could not be content with
this : it passed at once into action, and in this
guise prevailed to deface the fair front of the
Church with gashes of more bloody and barbarous inhumanity than ever marked the altars
of the Baals and Molochs of the most savage
heathen superstitions.

Another monstrous abuse born out of the
bosom of the Church, though not so directly,
is Sacerdotalism. I say not so directly, because the genius of Christianity is so distinctly
negative of all priesthood that, had there been

even an express prohibition of it, its contradiction to the whole tone of the New Testament could not have been more apparent.
Not more certainly are the sacrifices of the
Jewish law abolished in the sacrifice of Christ,
according to the Pauline theology, than the
Levitical priesthood stands abolished in the
priesthood of Christ and in the priesthood of
the individual members of his spiritual body
(2 Peter v. 9).[1] Whence, then, came our
Christian priesthood ? Partly, I suspect, as
the Jewish Sabbath was interpolated into the
Christian Lord's Day, from the nearness and
external similitude of the two things—the
presbyter being to the outward eye pretty
much the same as the priest was to the Jewish
worshippers ; partly from the self-importance
which is the besetting sin of all bodies of men
prominently planted in the social platform,
and which induces them to magnify their
vocation, and in doing so stilt their profes-

[1] In the διδαχή τῶν ἀποστόλων, c. xiii., the "prophets" are
said to be to Christians what the "high priests" were to the
Jews,—a phraseology which could not possibly have been used
had any priesthood, in the Hebrew sense, existed in the early
Church.

sional pride up into the attitude of a very stately and a very reputable virtue. The proper functions of the office-bearers of the early Christian Church, call them overseers, bishops, or what you will, were so honorable and so beneficent that, especially with an unlearned and unthinking people, the reverential respect due to the actors might easily pass into a superstitious belief in the mystical virtue of the operations of which they were the conductors ; and this ready submission on the part of the people, holding out a willing hand to the natural self-importance and potentiated self-estimate of the clerical body, resulted in a four-square system of sacerdotal control, sacerdotal virtue, and sacerdotal influence, to which we shall search for a parallel in vain through all the annals of Asiatic and African heathenism.   Nay, I can readily believe that those who can find a priesthood in the genius of the gospel and the apostolic institution of the Christian Church, will naturally be inclined to maintain that the superior power of the Gregories, Bonifaces, and Innocents of the medieval Church, as contrasted with anything that we read or know of the Egyptian, Hebrew, and Roman pontiffs, is the natural and necessary outcome of the superior excellence of the Christian religion ; and this, no doubt, is the only comfortable belief on which all forms of Christian sacerdotalism can repose.

So much for the corruptions of the Christian religion proceeding from what, in theological language, might be called the indwelling sin of the Church, unstimulated by any strong external seduction. But this seduction came. After three centuries of hardship, manfully endured in the school of adversity, the more severe trial of prosperity had to be gone through. The Church, which had been declared to be not of this world, and had stood face to face with the greatest political power the world ever knew in a position of sublime moral isolation, was now adopted by the State, and formed a bond of the most intimate connection with its hereditary persecutors. The starting-point of the oldest heathen social attitude, the identity of Church and State, seemed to be recalled ; and a Justinian on the shores of the Bosphorus seemed as really a head of the Church as a Menes or an Amenophis on the banks of the Nile. But under the outward likeness a radical difference lay concealed. As an essentially ethical society, with its own special credentials, its separate history, and its independent triumph, the Christian Church might form an alliance with a purely secular institution like the State, but it could not be absorbed or identified with it. That alliance might be made beneficially in various ways and on various terms; the civil magistrate might be proud to be called the friend and the brother of the Christian bishop, or he might humble himself to be its servant, but he never could be its master. The alliance therefore was, as it ought to be, all in favor of the spiritual body; the Church gained the civil power to execute its decrees and to patronize its missions; but a Christian State could never gain the right to dictate the creed or perform the functions of the Church. The idea that there is anything absolutely sinful, or necessarily pernicious, in the conception of an alliance between the

Church and the State, is one of those hyper-conscientious crotchets of modern British sectarianism at which the Muse of history can only smile. There can be no greater sin in an Established Church than in an Established University or an Established Royal Academy. Religion 'and Science and Art have their separate and well-marked provinces, in the administration of which they may wisely seek for the coöperation, though they will always jealously avoid the dictation, of the State. But, though there could be no sin in the Church receiving the right hand of fellowship from the State, there might be danger, and that of a very serious description. Nothing strikes a man so much in the reading of the New Testament as the little respect which it pays to riches and the pomp and pride of life, and worldly honors and dignities of all kinds. " *How can ye believe who receive honor one from another ?* " is a sentence that cuts very deep into the connection between the Church and State, which might readily mean the alliance of a secular institution, delighting in pomp and parade and glittering show, with

a religion of which, like the philosophy of the
porch, the most prominent feature was unworldliness, humility, and spirituality. Here
unquestionably was danger : an alliance in
which, as in an ill-consorted marriage, the
lower element was as likely to drag down the
higher as the higher to lift up the lower.
And so it actually happened. The Church
was secularized. Alongside of the hundred
and one monkeries of stolid asceticism and the
hundred and one mummeries of sacerdotal
ceremonialism, there grew up in the process
of the ages a consolidated hierarchy of such
concentrated, secular, and sacred potency that
the loftiest crowned heads of Europe ducked
beneath its shadow and quailed beneath its
ban. To understand this, we must take note
of the change by which the scattered presby-
ters of the primitive Church were gradually
massed into a strong aristocracy, which in
due season, after the fashion of the State,
found its key-stone in an ecclesiastical monarch. It was the wisdom of the founders of
the Christian Church not to lay down any
fixed norm of official administration, but to

leave all the external machinery of a purely
spiritual institution free to adapt itself to the
existing forms of society as time and circumstance and national genius might demand.
The form of government natural to the Church
in its earliest stages was democratic, with
a certain loose, ill-defined element of presi-
dential aristocracy. But in an age which
had bidden a long farewell both to the
spirit and the form of democracy in civil
administration, such a form of government
in the Church could not hope to maintain
itself. Under the influence of the magnifi-
cent autocracy of Rome in its decadence,
the simple overseer or superintendent (ἐπί-
σκοπος) of a remote provincial congregation
of believers gradually grew into a metropoli-
tan dignitary, and culminated in the wielder of
a secular sovereignty sitting in council with
the most influential monarchs of Europe. The
epiphany of an absolute monarch with a triple
tiara on his head when contrasted with the
simplicity and unworldliness of the primitive
bishops wears such a strange look that it has
been judged, especially in Protestant countries,

with a more sweeping severity than it deserved. As a mere form of government, no man can give any good reason why the Church should not be governed by a monarch as well as the State ; the bishop of Rome, as supreme head of the body of bishops all over Christendom, and guided by them as his habitual advisers, was at least as natural and as reasonable a guide for the direction of the conscience of Christendom in the Middle Ages as the Council of Protestants who at Dort, in the year 1618, condemned the greatest theologian and jurist of the day to pine in a Dutch prison, or the Assembly of Divines in Westminster who empowered the supreme magistrate to suppress the right of free thought in the breasts of all persons who were not prepared to set their seal to the damnatory dogmas of extreme Calvinism. Nay, so far from there being anything anti-Christian or anti-social in the Popedom as a form of Church government, we may safely say that in ages of general turmoil, confusion, and violence, the admitted supremacy of the visible head of a church founded on principles of peace and concilia-

tion could not act otherwise, than beneficially.
But when the person in whom this moral
supremacy was vested became the acknowl-
edged head of a secular princedom, the case
was altered. It was an unhappy day for the
Christian Church, the most unhappy day perhaps in its whole eventful history, when Pepin,
the ambitious minister of the last of the Mero-
vingian kings, in the year 751, contrived to get
out of Pope Zachary a spiritual sanction for
his usurpation of his master's throne. From
that moment the Church was doomed to a
blazing and brilliant, but a sure career of
downfall. The spiritual abetter of a secular
crime had to be rewarded for his pious sub-
serviency : he received the exarchate of Ra-
venna, and became a temporal prince. From
that time forward the head of the Christian
Church, who ought to have stood before the
world as a model of all purity, truthfulness,
peacefulness, and ethical nobility, was condemned to serve two masters, God and Mam-
mon, unworldly morality and worldly power,
which was impossible. From this time forward
there was not a single court intrigue in Europe,

nor a single plot of any knot of conspirators,
into whose counsels the supreme bishop of the
gospel of peace might not be dragged, or, what
is worse, into whose lawless and ungodly
machinations he might not be officially thrust-
ing himself, in order to preserve some accessory interest or gain some paltry advantage
altogether unconnected with his spiritual function. If there is any one element, always of
course excepting the element of gross sensuality and absolute villainy, which more than
another is adverse to the spirit of Evangelical
Christianity, it is the element of court intrigue,
political contention, and party feuds. In this
region love, which is the life of the regenerate
soul, cannot breathe; truth is put under ban;
lies flourish; conscience is smothered; and
low expediency everywhere takes the place of
lofty principle. So it fared not seldom with
the Popes; and much worse in the last degree; for wickedness, like everything that
lives, must live by growing, and the seed of
secular ambition which was sown in lies, will
grow to robbery, blossom in lust, and ripen
into murder. This anywhere, but specially

in Italy, where from the time of the patrician
Scipio, who suppressed the elder Gracchus,
the hot contenders for absolute power, in the
eager pursuit of their object, have never shrank
from the free use of the assassin's dagger and
the poisoner's bowl. In fact, if the love of
mere animal pleasure makes a man a beast, it
is the love of power that translates him into a
fiend ; and of this sort of human fiends Italian
history presents as appalling a register as can
be found anywhere in the annals of our race ;
and at the top of this register stand some of
the Popes, whose names are as prominent in
the story of ecclesiastical Rome as those of
Nero, Domitianus, and Heliogabalus are in the
story of the imperial decadence. When we
cast a rapid glance—for it deserves nothing
more—on the revolting record of the Roman
Popes in the age immediately preceding the
Reformation, we hear the solemn voice of history repeating again the maxim above quoted—
corruptio optimi pessima : when priests are
bad, they are very bad ; when the salt of the
gospel, which was meant to preserve the moral
life of society from putrescence, has lost its

savor, if not cast out, it is worse than use-
less—it becomes a poison.

Before proceeding to the modern history of
the Church, we ought to emphasize in a special
paragraph the fact that one unfortunate result
of the incorporation of the Church with the
State was that the Church was now in a position to request the State to lend its potent aid
in establishing the true doctrine of the gospel
and suppressing all heresies. That the State
had a right to do so no man doubted ; even in
democratic Greece free-thinking philosophers,
such as Anaxagoras, Diogenes, and Socrates,
were banished or suffered death on charges of
impiety ; and though, no doubt, political elements, as in the case of the Arminians in Hol-
land, worked along with the strictly religious
feeling to set the brand of atheism on those
men, there cannot be any doubt that where
the State and the Church were so essentially
one, persecutions for unauthorized religious
observances were perfectly legitimate, as indeed the memorable case of the forcible suppression of the Dionysiac mysteries, more than
two hundred years before the earliest of the

Christian martyrdoms in Rome, abundantly testifies. But there was a double horror in the religious persecution, after the establishment of Christianity, now inaugurated for the first time—the horror of a conduct so diametrically opposed to the spirit and the express injunction of the Founder of the Gospel, in whose defence it was practiced, and the horror also that what was now violently suppressed was not, as in the case of the Dionysiac mysteries, rather immoral practices than erroneous beliefs, but simply and nakedly metaphysical objections against metaphysical propositions in theology, which, whether true or false, could not be made the subject of State action, or, in my opinion at least, of ecclesiastical censure, without a flagrant violation of that law of charity which a large philosophy and a catholic Christianity equally enjoin. The banishment of Arius to Illyria, as the civil consequence of the formal signature of the Trinitarian creed by the decision of the Council of Nice in the year 325, though it made no small noise in the world in those days, was a very innocent overture to the barbarous dramas of fire and blood that were in after ages to be enacted on this evil precedent. There are many grand places rich with historical lessons in London, and not a few sad ones; but the saddest of all is Smithfield. I can never pace the stones of this memorable site, where our noblest Scot, Sir William Wallace, was disembowelled and quartered to gratify the vengeance of an imperious Norman, without thinking of the sad fate of the young and beautiful Anne Askew. This lady, the daughter of a knight of good family in Lincolnshire, under some of those stimulants of thought which were stirring up the stagnant traditions of medieval piety, had been led to conceive serious doubts with regard to the Scripture authority for some of the most universally received doctrines of the Roman Church. This pious scepticism coming to the ears of certain leading persons in Church and State, who, after the example of the Nicean doctors, considered it a sacred duty in matters pertaining to religion to tolerate no contradiction, first brought this lady before the Lord Chancellor, who tore her limb from limb on the rack, because she

would not say that she believed what she
could not believe without denying her senses,
and then dragged her to the blood-stained
pavement of Smithfield, where she was girt
with gunpowder bags and fenced with fagots,
to be burnt to death, as if the God of Christians were a second and enlarged edition of the
old Moloch of Palestine. And what was her
offence—beautiful, young, pure, and truth-
ful woman, not more than twenty-five years
of age—that she should be treated in this
worse than cannibalic style in the name of
the gospel of Jesus Christ? Simply that
Henry VIII., in that style of insolent masterdom which he showed so royally, and conceit-
ing himself, like a Scotch fool who came after
him, to be a considerable theologian, assumed
the right to put the stamp of absolute kingship on the doctrine of the Church that a piece
of bread, over which a priestly benediction
had been pronounced by a priest, was by the
mystical virtue of this benediction changed
into flesh, while the fair young lady persisted
in seeing nothing but bread. Let it be granted
that the lady was in the wrong and the church-

ly tradition right, it never could be right to
tear her flesh to shreds and to burn her bones
to ashes because she held an opinion which, to
say the least of it, looked as like the truth as
its opposite. How sad, how sorrowfully sad,
and what a commentary on what we are ever
and anon tempted to call poor, pitiful, pride-
ful, and presumptuous human nature, that
Christianity had at that time been more than
fifteen hundred years in the world, sitting in
high places, and walking with triumphal ban-
ners over the earth, and yet neither the princes
of the earth nor the rulers of the Church should
have retained even a slight echo of that reproof
from a mild Master to a zealous disciple, to
the effect that no man who knew the spirit of
the divine religion which He taught, would
ever propose to bring fire down from heaven
or up from hell to consume the unbeliever.

Such enormities in the doctrine and practice
of the Church, as we have indicated rather than
described, could lead to only one of two issues
—Reform or Revolution. The change brought
about, though contenting itself with the
milder name, was in fact the more drastic pro-

cedure. The European reformation of Martin Luther in 1517 was a revolution in the Church, much more radical and much more worthy of so strong a designation than the political revolution of 1688 in Great Britain. It is needless to recapitulate the causes of offence ; they were only too patent—insolence, secularity, sensuality, venality, idleness, vice, and worthlessness of every kind in the Church ; but there were two causes which, in addition to corruption from within, tended to open the ears of Christendom largely to the cry for Church reform. These were the stir in the intellectual movement from the days of the author of the Divine Comedy downward, enforced by the invention of printing in the middle of the fifteenth century, which was amply sufficient to become a danger to even a much less vulnerable creed than that which had satisfied the crude demands of medieval intelligence ; and, in the second place, the hostility which the insolence and ambition of Churchmen had roused in the secular magistracy—that is, not only the monarch and his official ministers, but the great body of the

higher nobility who found themselves ousted
from their place in the familiar counsels of the
monarch by the advocates and ambassadors of
a foreign potentate. Thus the two best friends
of every Established Church in its normal
state were converted into enemies; and the
natural indignation of the common people at
the licentious lives and gross venality of the
clergy was stimulated into an explosion by the
desire of the secular dignities to curb the pride
of the clergy, and, it might lightly happen
also, to rob them of part of their overgrown
wealth, nominally for the public good, really
for the aggrandizement of the Crown and the
nobility. The shameless nepotism of Pope
Sixtus IV., the flagitious lives and abhorrent
practices of the Borgias, more fit for a sensa-
tional melodrama in the lowest Parisian theatre
than for the home of a Christian bishop; the
military rage of a Julius, who turned the
Church of Christ into a travelling camp and
the bishop's crozier into a soldier's sword; the
literary dilettanteism of the Court of Leo X.,
more eager to distinguish itself by the elegant
trimming of Latin versicles than by apostolic

zeal and (hristian purity,—all this, so long as
it disported itself on Italian ground, the aristocracy of England and Scotland might have
continued to look on with indifference ; but
that the son of anybody or nobody, in a
county of unvalued clodhoppers, should jostle
them in the antechamber of the monarch, and
claim precedence in the hall of audience,
simply because he was the supple instrument
of an insolent Italian priest, this was not to be
borne ; and so the Reformation came, with the
mob of the lowest classes, the mass of the re-
spectable middle classes, the most influential
of the nobility, and the power of the Crown,
all in full cry against the ecclesiastical fox.
The revolution thus volcanically effected, and
known in history under the name of Protestantism, meant simply the right of every individual member of the Christian Church to take
the principles and the practice of his Church
directly from the original records of the
Church, without the intervention of any body
of authorized interpreters ; and the necessary
product of this right when exercised was first
to declare certain practices and doctrines that

had grown up in the Church through long centuries to be unauthorized departures from the
original simplicity and purity of the gospel ;
and, further, to deny that there existed in
the Christian Church, as originally consti-
tuted, any class or caste of men enjoying the
exclusive‘ privilege to perform sacred functions, and endowed with a divine virtue
to perform sacramental miracles by their
consecrating touch,—in a word, that there
was no priesthood, properly so called, in
the Reformed Christian Church. Nor is this
doctrine, as some may think, the teaching
only of the Helvetic confession, what certain
persons have been fond to call extreme Protestantism ; for, though the word priest has been
retained in the English prayer-book as a minister in sacred things of a particular grade and
exercising a particular function, the attempt
made by Archbishop Laud and the Romaniz-
ing party in the Reformed Church of England
to retain in the bosom of the Anglican Church
the ideas which the ancient Jews and the
Romish Christians attached to the word *priest*,
proved a signal failure ; and for the sacerdotal

despotism which it implied, as well as for the secular despotism which the priest advised and encouraged the unfortunate king to assert, the adviser and the advised justly lost their heads. Of all the teachings of Church history, from the Waldenses in the twelfth century down to the present hour, there is nothing more certain than this, that between Popery and Protestantism there is no middle term possible. They may agree, in fact they do agree, in many essential things, and in a few accidental ; but in the fundamental principle of Church administration they are diametrically opposed. The principle of the one is sacerdotal authority, absolute and unqualified ; the principle of the other is individual and congregational liberty. The one form of polity is a close oligarchy, the other either a free democracy or an aristocracy more or less penetrated by a democratic spirit.

The practical outcome of this great Protestant movement, in the midst of which we live, cannot fail to a reasonable eye to appear in the highest degree satisfactory. Never was the life of the Christian Church at once more intensely earnest and more expansively distributive than at the present moment. On the one hand, the Roman Church, wisely taught by the experience of the past, though obstinately cleaving to that stout conservatism of doctrine and ritual inherent in the very bones of all sacerdotal religions, has been, in the main, studious to avoid those causes of offence from which the great rupture proceeded. On the other hand, the Protestant Churches, shaken free from the distracting influence of sacerdotal assumption and secular ambition, have found themselves in a condition to permeate all classes of society with a moral virtue, of whose regenerative action Plato and Socrates, in their best hours, could not have dreamed. Some people, while gladly admitting the immense amount of social good that is done by the various sections of the Protestant Church, never cease to sigh for a lost ecclesiastical unity, and to lament the unseemly strifes that arise among those that should be possessed by one spirit and strive together for a common end. But the persons who speak thus are either sentimental weaklings, being Protestants, or are Romanists and sacerdotalists in their heart. Variety is the law of nature in the moral no less than in the physical world; and the absorption of all sects into one results in a stagnation which will never be found among moral beings, unless when produced by weakness of vital force from within, or unnatural suppression from above. The two dominant types of church polity recognized in this country since the Reformation—the Episcopal and the Presbyterian—of which the one boasts a more aristocratic intellectual culture, and the other a more fervid and forcible popular action, may well be allowed to exist together on a mutual understanding of giving and taking whatever is best in each, and thus, in apostolic language, provoking one another to love and to good works. Competition is for the public benefit as much in churches as in trades. Dissent from any dominant body, even though it may proceed from the exaggerated importance given to a secondary matter, will always produce the good result that the dominant body will thereby be stirred to

greater activity and greater watchfulness; so
that, in this view, we may lay it down as one
of the great lessons of history that the
best form of church government is a strong
establishment qualified by a strong dissent.
As to the proposals which have in recent times
been made for the formal separation of Church
and State, they bear on their face more of a
political than of a religious significance. Impartial history offers no countenance to the
notion that Established Churches, when well
flanked by dissent, and in an age when the
spiritual ruler has ceased to make the arm of
the State the tool of intolerance, are contrary
either to piety or to policy ; and in the desire
so loudly expressed at election contests to lay
violent hands on the valuable organism of
church agency existing in this country, the
venerated inheritance of many ages of patriotic
struggle, the student of history, with a chari-
table allowance for the best motives in not a
few, feels himself constrained to suspect in all
such movements no small admixture of secta-
rian jealousy, fussy religiosity, and domineer-
ing democracy. Christianity, of course, stands

in no need of an Established Church ; religion
existed for three hundred years in the church
without any State connection, and may exist
again ; but Christianity does, above all things,
abhor the stirring up of strife betwixt Church
and Church from motives of jealousy, envy, or
greed ; and, along with the highest philosophy
and the most far-sighted political wisdom,
must protest in the strongest terms against the
abolishing of a useful ethical institution to
gratify the insane lust of levelling in a mere
numerical majority.

The Church of the future, whether established or disestablished, or, as I think best,
both together, provoking one another to love
and to good works, has a great mission before
it, if it keep sharply in view the two lessons
which the teaching of eighteen centuries so
eloquently enforces. Our evangelists must re-
move from the van of their evangelic force all
that sharp fence of metaphysical subtlety
and scholastic dogma, which, being osten-
tatiously paraded in creeds and catechisms,
has given more just offence to those without than edification to those within the

Church; the gospel must be presented to the world with all that catholic breadth, kindly humanity, and popular directness which were its boast before it was laced and screwed into artificial shapes by the decrees of intolerant councils, and the subtleties of ingenious schoolmen. And, again, they must not allow the gospel to be handled, what is too often the case, as a mere message of hope and comfort in view of a future world ; but they must make it walk directly into the complex relations of modern society, and think that it has done nothing till the ideal of sentiment and conduct which it preached on Sunday has been more or less practiced on Monday. In fact, there ought to be less vague preaching on Sunday, and more specific and direct application through the week of gospel principle in various spheres of the intellectual and moral life of the community. If, in addition to this, our prophets of the pulpit take care to keep abreast of the intellectual movement of the age, so as not only to stir the world in sermons, but to guide them in the wisdom of daily life, they have nothing to fear from all

the windy artillery that the speculations of a
soulless physical science, the imaginations of
a dreamy socialism, or the dogmatism of a cold
philosophical formalism, can bring to bear upon
them. Let them grapple bravely with all
social problems, and prove whether Christianity, which has done so much to purify the
motives of individuals, may not be able also
to put a more effective steam into the machinery of society. If they shall fail here,
they will fail gloriously, having done their
best. It is not given to any people, however
great, to solve all problems. When Great
Britain shall have played out her part,
there will be scope enough in the process of
the ages for another stout social worker to
place the cornice on the edifice of which she
was privileged to raise the pillars.

ATLANTIS.

ATLANTIS: THE ANTEDILUVIAN WORLD. By IG-
NATIUS DONNELLY. Illustrated. 12mo, Cloth, $2 00.

Mr. Donnelly's theory is an ingenious one, and is well fortified by argu-
ments drawn from geology and history, from prehistoric relics, from traditions, and from manners, languages, and customs of widely separated
nations. His theory offers a plausible explanation for many puzzling
discoveries of the philosophers, and his book will give a fresh impulse to
historic and prehistoric research.—*Philadelphia Inquirer.*

Mr. Ignatius Donnelly has written a unique and interesting argument to
prove that the legend of Atlantis is based upon fact, and that it tells of
the first and one of the greatest of civilized nations, which a terrible con-
vulsion of nature obliterated.—*Congregationalist,* Boston.

All of this is very startling, but the author has made out a case which,
if not convincing, is at least interesting and wonderfully plausible. His
book shows, throughout, wide reading, logical clearness, and careful
thought, and the work cannot fail to interest by the vast accumulation of
out-of-the-way information it contains.—*Saturday Evening Gazette,* Boston.

This is a most remarkable book, entertaining, instructive, and fascinat-
ing to a degree. . . . A book well worth reading. The world will never
tire of the story of the lost Atlantis and of speculations in regard to it.
It has been the theme of the poet and philosopher. Now it is brought
to the test of science.—*Brooklyn Union-Argus.*

If any one should get the impression that Mr. Donnelly's book is a
foolish one, he will make a great mistake. There is an immense amount
of knowledge accumulated, and some of his views have much more beneath them than notions in science which have wide prevalence. Whatever may be thought of his conclusions, the facts he has assembled with
regard to the Deluge and the several traditions concerning it, his com-
parisons of the Old and New World civilizations, his analysis of the my-
thologies of the Old World, and his discernment and selection of Atlan-
tean colonies make up a marvellously interesting book.—*Christian Advo-
cate,* N. Y.

It has a strange interest to the general reader as well as to scientific
students.—*Evangelist,* N. Y.

He must have the credit, however, of giving to the public the most
original volume of the season.—*The Congregationalist,* Boston.

The book contains matter food for thought from the first page to the
last, and its subject is so consequential that, if its major propositions can
be considered proven, some of the most perplexing problems which the
history of the human race offers to the investigator will, for the first time
since the revival of civilization, be put in the way of satisfactory solution.
—*Evening Telegraph,* Philadelphia.

PUBLISHED BY HARPER & BROTHERS, NEW YORK.

CHARLES NORDHOFF'S WORKS.

POLITICS FOR YOUNG AMERICANS. By CHARLES NORDHOFF. 16mo,
Half Leather, 75 cents ; Paper, 40 cents.

It is a book that should be in the hand of every American boy and girl. This
book of Mr. Nordhoff's might be learned by heart. Each word has its value;
each enumerated section has its pith. It is a complete system of political science,
economical and other, as applied to our American system.—*N. Y. Herald.*

CALIFORNIA : A Book for Travellers and Settlers. By CHARLES NORD-
HOFF. A New Edition. With Maps and Illustrations. 8vo, Cloth,
$2 00.

Mr. Nordhoff's plan is to see what is curious, important, and true, and then to
tell it in the simplest manner. Herodotus is evidently his prototype. Strong
sense, a Doric truthfulness, and a very earnest contempt for anything like pretension or sensationalism, and an enthusiasm none the less agreeable because
straitened in its expression, are his qualities.—*N. Y. Evening Post.*

THE COMMUNISTIC SOCIETIES OF THE UNITED STATES; from
Personal Visit and Observation : including Detailed Accounts of the
Economists, Zoarites, Shakers ; the Amana, Oneida, Bethel, Aurora,
Icarian, and other Existing Societies ; their Religious Creeds, Social
Practices, Numbers, Industries, and Present Condition. By CHARLES
NORDHOFF. Illustrated. 8vo, Cloth, $4 00.

Mr. Nordhoff has derived his materials from personal observation, having vis-
ited the principal Communistic societies in the United States, and taken diligent
note of the peculiar features of their religions creed and practices, their social and
domestic customs, and their industrial and financial arrangements. * * * With his
exceptionally keen powers of perception, and his habits of practised observation,
he could not engage in such an inquiry without amassing a fund of curious
information. In stating the results of his investigations, he writes with exem-
plary candor and impartiality, though not without the exercise of just and sound
discrimination.—*N. Y. Tribune.*

CAPE COD AND ALL ALONG SHORE: STORIES. By CHARLES NORD-
HOFF. 12mo, Cloth, $1 50 ; 4to, Paper, 15 cents.

Light, clever, well-written sketches.—*N. Y. Times.*
A lively and agreeable volume, full of humor and incident.—*Boston Transcript.*

GOD AND THE FUTURE LIFE. The Reasonableness of Christianity.
By CHARLES NORDHOFF. 16mo, Cloth, $1 00.

Mr. Nordhoff's object is not so much to present a religious system as to give
practical and sufficient reasons for every-day beliefs. He writes strongly, clearly,
and in the vein that the people understand.—*Boston Herald.*

PUBLISHED BY HARPER & BROTHERS, NEW YORK.

☞ HARPER & BROTHERS *will send the above works by mail, postage prepaid, to any
part of the United States or Canada, on receipt of the price.*

AMERICAN POLITICAL IDEAS,

Viewed from the Standpoint of Universal History. By JOHN
FISKE. pp. 158. 12mo, Cloth, $1 00.

Mr. Fiske is one of the few Americans who is able to exercise
a dispassionate judgment upon questions which have been the
cause of quarrels between parties and sections. Mr. Fiske has a
calm way of considering our modern ideas from the standpoint
of universal history.—*N. Y. Journal of Commerce.*

We know of no treatise concerning American history which is
likely to exercise larger or better influence in leading Americans to
read between the lines of our country's annals. * * * The little
book is so direct and simple in the manner of its presentation of
truth, so attractive in substance, that its circulation is likely to
be wide. Its appeal is as directly to the farmer or mechanic as
to the philosophic student of politics or history.—*N. Y. Commercial
Advertiser.*

There is not a line in the entire work which is not laden with
the richest fruits of a trained and powerful intellect.—*Commercial
Bulletin,* Boston.

When Mr. Fiske comes to discuss American history by the comparative method, he enters a field of special and vital interest to
all who have ever taken up this method of study. Our history, as
the author says, when viewed in this broad and yet impartial way,
acquires a new dignity. There is no need to say that Mr. Fiske's
pages are worthy of the most careful study.—*Brooklyn Union.*

From this point of view the consideration of the political ideas
of this country becomes something more than a mere study of
history; it constitutes a page of philosophy, a social study of the
most transcendant importance. Such is the spirit with which
Prof. Fiske handles his subject. He shows how our institutions
have grown and developed from the past, how they have a firm
basis in nature, and how they must develop in the future. The
lectures are important reading; they are also pleasant reading, for
the literary style of Prof. Fiske is exceptionally pure, clear, and
graceful.—*Boston Gazette.*

A volume of great interest, and illustrates very happily some of
the fundamental ideas of American politics by setting forth their
relations to the general history of mankind. * * * We heartily
commend this little volume to such of our readers as desire to en-
large their ideas and views of the political principles underlying the
foundations of our system of government.—*Christian at Work,* N. Y.

PUBLISHED BY HARPER & BROTHERS, NEW YORK.

NEWCOMB'S POLITICAL ECONOMY,

PRINCIPLES OF POLITICAL ECONOMY. By
SIMON NEWCOMB, LL.D., Professor of Mathematics,
U. S. Navy, Professor in the Johns Hopkins University, Author of "Popular Astronomy," &c.   pp. xvi.,
548.   8vo, Cloth, $2 50.

Nothing so good is, that we know of, to be found elsewhere.   Every section, we might almost say every page, abounds in instruction. . . . The book
should be more than read; it should be carefully studied, and students who
make themselves masters of the problems set for them in the illustrations
and exercises interspersed among the chapters would know more of the
subject than many of the avowed professors of the science in our colleges.
—*N. Y. Commercial Advertiser.*

It is timely, useful, and invaluable.   The questions considered are now
before the citizens of the United States for their decision.   More valuable
help than that afforded by this volume towards a complete understanding
of these questions and towards conclusions that will promote national
prosperity, is not to be found.—*Christian Intelligencer, N. Y.*

In the present volume Professor Newcomb has directed his great powers
of analysis to the difficult subject of political economy.   Whatever such a
man says about anything he never fails to make clear.   The reader of this
exposition of a science little understood will never have the slightest doubt
of Professor Newcomb's meaning.—*N. Y. Journal of Commerce.*

In a broad and profound consideration of the subject on both its scientific and practical side; in an engaging candor, a mathematical clearness
and precision, and a weighty grasp of the great subject and its relations,
no previous work on political economy can compare with this by Dr. Newcomb.—*Boston Evening Traveller.*

The merit of Professor Newcomb's treatment consists in thorough
knowledge and mastery of the subject, in its freedom from partisanship,
its simple and clear logical statement and apt illustration, and in its general suggestiveness to the reader to inquire and think for himself from
what is given him.   Through this combination of essentials to instruction
and independent investigation it has the power to accomplish more than
any other work.—*Boston Globe.*

PUBLISHED BY HARPER & BROTHERS, NEW YORK.

☞ *The above work sent by mail, postage prepaid, to any part of the United States
or Canada, on receipt of the price.*

BY ALBERT STICKNEY.

DEMOCRATIC GOVERNMENT. A Study of Politics. By ALBERT STICKNEY. pp. 170. 12mo, Cloth, $1 00.

It has the merit of independent, earnest, and original conviction. It is throughout thoroughly American, and shows the democratic training that has made New England life so forceful in all parts of this country. ... The book will arouse interest because of its freshness and evident and sensible patriotism.—*Philadelphia Times.*

Mr. Stickney is thoroughly convinced that our present Constitution does not meet the requirements of this nation, and his reasons for so thinking he has given with great energy and clearness. ... Mr. Stickney is an unusually stimulating and suggestive writer.—*Rochester Democrat and Chronicle.*

The exposition of the evil of professional politicians, of ring rule politics, and of divided responsibility should be read by every citizen.—*N. Y. Herald.* •

It is the aim of this volume to show that there is a remedy, and that this is in simply returning to a truly popular representative government. ... The volume will surely be accepted as a valuable contribution to the political thought of the time.—*N. Y. Times.*

A clear, vigorous discussion of practical politics. ... It is one of many signs that people are thinking to the point, as well as a help to students to formulate their own vague notions.—*Atlantic Monthly,* Boston.

An intelligently and forcibly considered study in politics, deals temperately, justly, vigorously, and from the stand-point of a consistent and conscientious Democrat, with the principles, precepts, and practice of democracy in its intended purity and impartial administration of justice.—*New Orleans Times-Democrat.* •

A TRUE REPUBLIC. By ALBERT STICKNEY. 12mo, Cloth, $1 00.

Mr. Stickney writes well and forcibly, and some of his propositions are undeniably true. ... His elegantly made and interesting book will be classed with the Utopia of Sir Thomas More and the Republic of Plato.—*N. Y. Evening Mail.*

Mr. Stickney's book will be found very suggestive. He sketches the different kinds of government people have lived under, and reviews our own. Every thinking American should read it.—*N. Y. Commercial Advertiser.*

PUBLISHED BY HARPER & BROTHERS, NEW YORK.

CAIRNES'S WORKS ON POLITICAL ECONOMY

SOME LEADING PRINCIPLES OF POLITICAL ECONOMY NEWLY EXPOUNDED. By J. E. CAIRNES, LL.D., late Emeritus Professor of Political Economy in University College, London. Crown 8vo, Cloth, $2 50.

It is with great pleasure that we welcome another contribution to Political Economy from the ablest living representative of the school of Ricardo and Mill. Mr. Cairnes aims at restating and modifying some of the doctrines which have hitherto passed muster as established principles. He brings to the task a remarkable power of sustained and accurate thought upon topics which are apt to bewilder an ordinary brain, and a capacity for lucid expression which is hardly less rare and admirable.—*Saturday Review*, London.

It not only throws new light on some of the most important problems of the science, but it entirely recasts the theory of cost of production, and thereby clears away, to a great extent, the mists and fogs by which the doctrines of international trade and international values are surrounded. ... The most important contribution which political economy has received for many years.—*Athenæum*, London.

THE CHARACTER AND LOGICAL METHOD OF POLITICAL ECONOMY. By J. E. CAIRNES, LL.D. 12mo, Cloth, $1 50.

Mr. Cairnes has rendered a great service to the literature of political economy in bringing out a second and greatly enlarged edition of this remarkable work. The present volume has received so many and such valuable additions that it will be read with almost as much interest as if it were an entirely new work. The general purpose of the book, which is to show that the deductive method is that which should be adopted in the pursuit of economic investigations, is dealt with by Mr. Cairnes in a most masterly and conclusive manner.—*Examiner*, London.

The lucidity and logical coherence of Professor Cairnes's writings render them admirable text-books for students, as well as useful for more mature thinkers.—*Saturday Review*, London.

No economical writer in England has, since Mill, commanded so much of public attention and respect.—*Nation*, N. Y.

PUBLISHED BY HARPER & BROTHERS, NEW YORK.

☞ *The above works sent by mail, postage prepaid, to any part of the United States or Canada, on receipt of the price.*

VALUABLE WORKS ON POLITICAL SCIENCE.

FISH'S PARLIAMENTARY LAW. American Manual of Parliamentary Law; or, The Common Law of Deliberative Assemblies. Systematically Arranged for the Use of the Parliamentarian and the Novice. By GEORGE T. FISH. 16mo, Cloth, 50 cents; Leather Tucks, $1 00.

NEWCOMB'S A B C OF FINANCE. The A B C of Finance; or, The Money and Labor Questions Familiarly Explained to Common People, in Short and Easy Lessons. By SIMON NEWCOMB, LL.D. 32mo, Paper, 25 cents.

GUERNSEY'S THE WORLD'S OPPORTUNITIES. The World's Opportunities, and How to Use Them; A View of the Industrial Progress of our Country; A Consideration of its Future Development; A Study of the Spheres of Woman's Work, and Estimates of the Rewards which Art and Science, Invention and Discovery, have in Store for Human Endeavor, with an Analysis of the Conditions of Present and Prospective Prosperity. 620 Pages, embracing 150 Different Subjects, with Comprehensive Tables of Statistics. By ALFRED H. GUERNSEY, Ph.D. Richly Illustrated. English Cloth, Emblematic Design, $4 75; Full Sheep (Library Style), Marbled Edges, $5 75; Half Morocco, Gilt Edges, $7 00. (*Sold only by Subscription.*)

WELLS'S ROBINSON CRUSOE'S MONEY. Robinson Crusoe's Money; or, The Remarkable Financial Fortunes and Misfortunes of a Remote Island Community. Fiction Founded upon Fact. By DAVID A. WELLS. Illustrated by THOMAS NAST. 8vo, Paper, 50 cents.

OLD-WORLD QUESTIONS AND NEW-WORLD ANSWERS. By DANIEL PIDGEON, F.G.S., Assoc. Inst. C. E. 12mo, Paper, 25 cents.

ATKINSON'S LABOR AND CAPITAL. Labor and Capital Allies, not Enemies. By EDWARD ATKINSON. 32mo, Paper, 20 cents.

PUBLISHED BY HARPER & BROTHERS, NEW YORK.

☞ *Any of the above works sent by mail, postage prepaid, to any part of the United States or Canada, on receipt of the price.*

WHAT SOCIAL CLASSES OWE TO EACH OTHER.

By WILLIAM GRAHAM SUMNER, Professor of Political and Social Science in Yale College. 16mo, Cloth, 60 cents.

There is no page of the book that is not weighty with meaning. The argument that runs through it is like a chain, strongly welded, link on to link. * * * Prof. Sumner gives clear, pointed, and powerful utterance to much social and political wisdom. The teaching of the book is just of that sort which is most needed by the young America of to-day.—*Boston Commonwealth.*

The conclusions he reaches are substantially unanswerable. * * * No more important doctrine than this can well be proclaimed, and our country owes a debt of gratitude to whoever will proclaim it in the sturdy style of this book. We need not despair of the Republic while our young men are fed upon such meat as this. Whether they adopt his conclusions or not, they cannot fail to be stimulated by his reasoning.—*The Nation,* N. Y.

Prof. Sumner has selected a subject of great interest and importance, and has treated it with ingenuity, penetration, and originality, and in a plain, homely, pungent, and effective style.—*Brooklyn Union.*

His little book is full of excellent maxims of conduct formed on the manly principle of doing hard work and letting everybody have a fair chance. * * * These eleven short chapters are undoubtedly the ablest of recent contributions to matters on which much unprofitable ink is spent.—*N. Y. Times.*

This ˙ .me contains a most instructive discussion of certain economic questions which are of living interest touching upon the duties of the State to classes or individuals embraced in it.—*Boston Globe.*

The style is bright and racy, and the argument is allowed to lose none of its force by the use of technical terms. The book is suggestive, and will be found helpful to those who desire to reach correct conclusions on subjects of practical importance.—*Christian at Work,* N. Y.

Prof. Sumner has enforced in very few and very simple words some of the most important and most neglected principles of political and social economy; has exposed, with temperate but none the less telling sarcasm, the most absurd but not least popular crotchets of modern philanthropic enthusiasm.—*Saturday Review,* London.

PUBLISHED BY HARPER & BROTHERS, NEW YORK.

☛ HARPER & BROTHERS *will send the above work by mail, postage prepaid, to any part of the United States or Canada, on receipt of the price.*

www.ingramcontent.com/pod-product-compliance
Lightning Source LLC
Chambersburg PA
CBHW030614270326
41927CB00007B/1175